ENTERTAINING

with Disney

ENTERTAINING

EXCEPTIONAL EVENTS

From Mickey Mouse to *Moana*!

AMY CROUSHORN

INSIGHT
EDITIONS

San Rafael, California

Contents

Introduction

Who says Disney is just for kids? Not us! If there's an adult on Earth who doesn't laugh at a good Mickey Mouse cartoon or sing along to *The Little Mermaid* or cry when Moana returns the Heart of Te Fiti, then we have different ideas of fun. Disney transcends age, delighting the youngest kid to the most sophisticated adult. And adults love to entertain.

When it comes to entertaining, the experts always start with a theme—one that complements and enhances the event you're celebrating, bringing a little extra magic to a special occasion. And no one does magic like Disney. Hosting a Disney party is a great way to get everyone into a fun, festive mood, infusing your party with a special atmosphere of joy, romance, and nostalgia. There's a Disney theme for every event, from casual birthday parties and barbecues to fancy dinner parties to special occasions like baby showers and bridal showers. And all it takes to pull it together is a little planning, a little creativity, and a little hard work. Tiana would approve!

Celebrate life's magical moments with your favorite Disney characters, using these complete instructions to plan and host the parties of your dreams. From a romantic *Little Mermaid* bridal shower to a wickedly fun Disney villains Halloween party, these comprehensive guides will help you design invitations, craft decor, build the menu, decorate the event space, plan games and activities, create favors, and more. While these party plans pair a specific Disney character with a specific occasion, feel free to tweak a party to suit your event. Make *your* dreams come true and throw a *Lion King* birthday party or a *Frozen* baby shower.

With this book, you'll have everything you need to entertain with Disney.

How to Use This Book

This book is divided into eleven chapters containing the blueprints for eleven unique parties based on classic Disney characters. Each chapter is divided into three main sections:

For the Menu

The foundation of any party. This section includes recipes and ideas for the party's food and drink. Some are quick and easy, while others let you show off your culinary greatness.

For the Space

It's crafting time! This section includes easy DIY projects for room and table decor, such as centerpieces, posters, place settings, and other special decorations.

For Fun

Every party should include a little something extra for fun. Depending on the party, it could be a game, activity, playlist, favor, or invitation.

In addition to the three main sections, a guide to putting it all together wraps up each party plan. This is a timeline of what to do when, starting from two weeks ahead of the party and going right up to when the first guest arrives. Each portion of our timeline lists which tasks to focus on so even the least-experienced party planners can pull everything together without missing a detail.

Each recipe, project, or activity includes step-by-step instructions and a full list of ingredients and supplies. We use common ingredients and everyday tools, but for some of the crafts, we recommend using a cutting machine. This handy tool should be familiar to most home crafters, but if it isn't, no worries! We always include alternative methods for completing the projects.

Of course a party is more than a menu and a couple of crafts. It's the little touches that bring it together. To that end, we've photographed each of these parties in detail to serve as both guide and inspiration, with a ton of close-up shots to catch every special detail, from the tablecloths to the lighting to the flowers. In some cases, we've even included in-process photography of individual crafts to help you visualize how the project comes together.

The parties featured in this book are templates, and you can stick to them as closely as you feel comfortable. If you're new to the world of party planning and you want to do things by the book, that's okay! If you're a more experienced host and you know that a particular drink would be extra delicious if you just added one ingredient, then go for it. Have fun playing around with your own customizations to accommodate your dietary needs and personal taste.

When it comes to planning a good party, we believe in making it magical and easy at the same time. That's why this book includes a special bonus: Many of the signs, cards, name tags, and other printed ephemera featured in this book are actually custom printable templates. No more worrying about the quality of your calligraphy for your menus or place settings. Simply download the templates, customize them for your party, and print! All templates are free and available for download at **www.insighteditions.com/disneyparties**. Please refer to this URL when you see the ● symbol throughout this book.

Ready to dive in? Let's make some Disney party magic!

Cinderella
"Stroke of Midnight" New Year's Eve Party

Cinderella
"Stroke of Midnight" New Year's Eve Party

EVENT OVERVIEW

FOR THE MENU
- Royal Roast Beef Crostini
- Jaq and Gus's Cheese Nibbles
- Sparkling Gelatin Squares
- Bibbidi-Bobbidi-Blue Velvet Cupcakes
- Midnight Magic Punch

FOR THE SPACE
- Pumpkin Carriage Punch Bowl
- Glass Slipper Centerpiece
- Bluebird Backdrop

FOR FUN
- "At Midnight I Turn into a . . ." Party Board
- Royal Invitations

New Year's Eve is a special night: a night to be brave, to take a risk, to make plans, or even to make a wish. It's also the perfect night to put on a gorgeous dress, kick up your heels, and have a ball while you count down to midnight. Suffice to say the heroine behind this party knew a thing or two about keeping an eye on the clock! So gather all your most eligible friends, and put on your best shoes. It's time for a *Cinderella* "Stroke of Midnight" New Year's Eve Party.

This party is full of enough sparkle to put Cinderella's ball gown to shame: Guests will marvel at your glittery tablecloth, glass slipper centerpiece, and delicious Sparkling Gelatin Squares. The color palette is Cinderella blue, with touches of white and lots of silver and gold. Of course, we haven't left out Cinderella's animal friends; fun callouts to Jaq, Gus, and the rest of the gang are sprinkled throughout the menu, the table, and the decor. And don't forget the clock—keep one front and center so you can count down the minutes to midnight and the New Year!

(CLOCKWISE FROM TOP LEFT) Midnight Magic Punch; Glass Slipper Centerpiece; Bibbidi-Bobbidi-Blue Velvet Cupcakes; Pumpkin Carriage Punch Bowl; Jaq and Gus's Cheese Nibbles; "At Midnight I Turn into a . . ." Party Board

At
Midnight
I turn into a...

unicorn   mouse

pumpkin

a princess   PARTY
                 ANIMAL

ROYAL ROAST BEEF CROSTINI

- **Crostini bread slices**
- **Savory spreadable cheese in the flavor of your choice**
- **Roast beef, sliced**
- **Pepper jelly**
- **Green onions, sliced, for garnishing**

1. Spread each crostini slice with cheese and top with a slice of roast beef.
2. Add a small dollop of pepper jelly to each slice, and garnish with sliced green onions.

JAQ AND GUS'S CHEESE NIBBLES

- **Cheese crisps**
- **Blackberries**
- **Chèvre**
- **Honey**
- **Fresh thyme**

1. Spread cheese crisps out on your serving platter.
2. Spread each crisp with chèvre.
3. Add one blackberry on top of the chèvre and drizzle honey on top. Garnish with a few leaves of fresh thyme.

SPARKLING GELATIN SQUARES

YIELD: 8 SERVINGS

- **Four ¼-ounce packets unflavored gelatin**
- **2 cups cold water**
- **1¼ cups sugar**
- **2½ cups sparkling grape juice**
- **1 cup club soda**

1. Boil 1½ cups of the water.

2. In the meantime, in a mixing bowl, sprinkle 4 packets of unflavored gelatin over the remaining ½ cup cold water. Let stand for 1 minute.

3. Add the 1½ cups boiling water to the mixture, stirring constantly until granules are completely dissolved.

4. Add sugar to a separate mixing bowl, and pour gelatin mixture over the top. Stir the mixture well until sugar dissolves.

5. Let cool until no longer hot, then stir in sparkling grape juice and club soda.

6. Pour mixture into an 11-by-13-inch baking dish. Cover and chill in refrigerator for three hours or until set.

7. Once set, cut gelatin into bite-size squares and serve.

Note

There will be bubbles from the sparkling grape juice when you pour the mixture into the dish. That's okay! It creates a beautiful look to your gelatin when it cools.

BIBBIDI-BOBBIDI-BLUE VELVET CUPCAKES

YIELD: 24 CUPCAKES

CUPCAKES:

- 1 cup unsalted butter, room temperature
- 1⅓ cups granulated sugar
- 3 large eggs, room temperature
- ¼ cup canola oil
- 2 teaspoons vanilla extract
- ⅔ cup buttermilk
- Blue food coloring to desired color
- 2½ cups cake flour
- 1½ teaspoons baking powder
- ¼ teaspoon baking soda
- ½ teaspoon salt

FROSTING:

- 1 cup butter, room temperature
- 1 cup cream cheese, room temperature
- 4 cups powdered sugar
- 1 teaspoon vanilla extract

DECORATIONS:

- Blue fondant, cut into stars
- Edible glitter
- Silver sprinkles

DISNEY FUN FACT

The scene when Cinderella's Fairy Godmother transforms her torn dress into a beautiful ball gown is said to be Walt Disney's favorite piece of animation ever.

TO MAKE THE CUPCAKES:

1. Preheat oven to 350°F. Add cupcake liners to a 12-count cupcake pan. Set aside.

2. Using a hand mixer, cream butter and sugar in a small bowl until light and fluffy.

3. Add the eggs one at a time, thoroughly beating each one into the batter before adding the next. Add oil and vanilla extract and mix well.

4. In a separate bowl, pour in the buttermilk and slowly add blue food coloring until you reach your desired shade of blue. Set aside.

5. Sift together flour, baking powder, baking soda, and salt in medium bowl.

6. Add a third of the flour mixture to the wet ingredients and beat on low with hand mixer. Add half of the buttermilk to the batter, continuing to beat. Repeat this process, alternating another third of the flour mixture with the other half of the buttermilk until all ingredients are combined.

7. Divide the batter evenly between the cups on the prepared tray, filling each one ¾ full. Bake for 20 to 25 minutes.

8. Remove the cupcakes and place them on a rack to cool. Repeat for the second dozen. When the cupcakes are cooled, prepare the frosting.

TO MAKE THE FROSTING:

1. Combine butter and cream cheese in a mixing bowl, and beat for 2 to 3 minutes, until fluffy.

2. Add sugar, 1 cup at a time, and vanilla, and mix until smooth.

FOR ASSEMBLY:

1. Place the frosting in a large piping bag fit with a large piping tip. Push the frosting down into the bag. Pipe the frosting onto the cupcakes.

2. Decorate the frosted cupcakes with blue fondant stars, edible glitter, and silver sprinkles.

MIDNIGHT MAGIC PUNCH

YIELD: 12 SERVINGS

- **Two 750-milliliter bottles sparkling white grape juice, chilled**
- **3 cups blue tropical punch, chilled**
- **One 33.8-ounce bottle club soda, chilled**
- **Rock candy swizzle stick for garnishing**

Combine chilled juice, punch, and club soda in punch bowl. Serve with rock candy swizzle sticks for garnishing.

PUMPKIN CARRIAGE PUNCH BOWL

- **White pumpkin-shaped bowl**
- **Small cake stand**
- **Pumpkin Carriage Vinyl Templates** ⬇
- **Gold vinyl, or gold paint pen**
- **Cutting machine (optional)**
- **2 small pumpkins, real or decorative**
- **Hot glue gun**
- **Gold floral spray**

1. Place a pumpkin-shaped bowl on top of a small cake stand. If you don't have a pumpkin-shaped bowl, you can use any punch bowl and spray-paint it white. Be sure to paint only the outside of the bowl so the inside remains food safe.

2. Download the Pumpkin Carriage Vinyl Templates from our online resources. These templates are for the decorative vinyl elements that create the carriage door and window frames. ⬇

3. Using your cutting machine and the templates, cut out the frames from gold vinyl.

4. Place two small pumpkins on their sides next to the cake stand to look like the carriage wheels. We used gold foil candles in the shape of pumpkins, but you can spray-paint real pumpkins or craft pumpkins. Secure these to the side of the cake plate if needed using hot glue.

5. Create vine tendrils to the small pumpkins using a gold floral spray, and attach foliage to the underside of your cake plate using hot glue. Shape these to give the feel of the pumpkin vine tendrils that frame Cinderella's carriage and wheels.

6. On the day of your party, set your Pumpkin Carriage Punch Bowl on the table, and use it to serve your signature drink!

Tip

If you don't own a cutting machine, use the template for inspiration, and draw the windows and door onto the side of the bowl using a gold paint pen.

GLASS SLIPPER CENTERPIECE

- Wide satin ribbon chair sash
- Sewing machine
- Thread matching the color of the sash
- Poly-fill stuffing
- 4 gold tassels
- Plastic "glass" slipper
- Hot glue gun (optional)

1. Fold sash over on itself, so the right sides are facing each other. Trim fabric to create a square-shaped pillow.
2. Sew around three edges. Sew part of the fourth edge, leaving a 3-inch opening so you can stuff the pillow.
3. After sewing edges, turn fabric right side out and stuff the pillow to desired fullness.
4. Sew the opening closed.
5. Sew a gold tassel at each corner by hand, or attach using a hot glue gun.
6. Place glass slipper on top of the finished pillow. This will make a lovely centerpiece for your table.

BLUEBIRD BACKDROP

- 36-by-48-inch foam core board
- 1½ yards patterned fabric
- Masking tape
- Satin ribbon chair sash
- Hot glue gun
- Bluebird Template ⬇
- Blue card stock
- Several lengths of satin ribbon
- Happy New Year banner
- Adhesive picture-hangers
- Clear string
- Clock

1. Wrap foam core board with fabric, and secure to back side with masking tape.
2. Attach chair sash to top of fabric-covered board with hot glue.
3. Download the Bluebirds Template from our online resources and print on blue card stock. Cut out the bluebirds and set aside. ⬇
4. Glue a length of satin ribbon to the back of each bird's mouth so it looks like they are carrying the ribbon for Cinderella's dress.
5. Attach bluebirds and ribbon to corners of the board over the chair sash using hot glue.
6. Hang a Happy New Year banner over the chair sash.
7. Use adhesive picture-hangers to attach your backdrop to the wall over your appetizer table.
8. Use clear string to hang your clock on the backdrop.

DISNEY FUN FACT

Cinderella was nominated for three Academy Awards®: Best Sound, Best Original Score, and Best Original Song ("Bibbidi-Bobbidi-Boo").

"AT MIDNIGHT I TURN INTO A . . ." PARTY BOARD

At midnight, Cinderella's carriage turns back into a pumpkin. What do you turn into at midnight? Display this board somewhere where your guests can contribute their own suggestions . . . the sillier, the better!

- **Blue foam core board**
- **Gold frame**
- **Metal ruler**
- **Cutting mat**
- **Masking tape**
- **"At Midnight I Turn into a . . ." Template** ⬇
- **Gold card stock**
- **Cutting machine (optional)**
- **Spray glue**
- **Gold paint pen or marker**

1. Cut blue foam core board to size to fit your frame using a metal ruler and cutting mat. Our board is 16 by 20 inches.

2. Secure board inside frame using masking tape on the backside of the frame.

3. Download our "At Midnight I Turn into a . . ." Template from our online resources. Use your cutting machine to cut the text out of gold card stock. If you don't have a cutting machine, use our file as inspiration, and handwrite the phrase in gold paint pen or marker. ⬇

4. Attach the phrase you have cut out to the board using spray glue.

5. Display your framed board in a prominent spot along with a gold paint pen or marker, so your guests can fill in the board with their answers. Have fun!

ROYAL INVITATIONS

In *Cinderella*, every eligible maiden is summoned to attend the ball by royal command. Send out your own royal summons with these printable invitations that you can edit with your own party details.

- **Royal Invitation Template** ⬇
- **White card stock**
- **Gold envelopes (size A7)**
- **Gold confetti**

1. Download the Royal Invitation Template from our online resources and edit to include your party details. ⬇
2. Print your invitations on white card stock and cut out.
3. Place invitations in gold envelopes, along with a handful of gold confetti.
4. Send out your invites at least two weeks ahead of your party.

The royal ball awaits.

𝒴our presence is requested at a royal celebration.

Join us for a Stroke of Midnight New Year's Eve party.
By royal command, every eligible maiden (and gent) is to attend.

December 31, 2020
At 8 o'clock in the evening
Cinderella's Castle
1234 Palace Lane
RSVP to grandduke@thepalace.com

TWO OR MORE WEEKS BEFORE:

Send out invitations to your friends! There's something special about receiving an actual paper invitation, and this party's Royal Invitation Template makes it easy. Simply download, edit, and print out the invitations, and then send them by mail. For an extra special touch, deliver them by hand. This is also the time to purchase all of the craft supplies you will need for this party. Order a gold sequin tablecloth (this really makes a statement on your New Year's table!) and blue chair sashes for your backdrop and pillow craft. It is best to allow a couple of weeks for shipping for these items.

ONE WEEK BEFORE:

Gather your decor and your serving ware. When selecting your serving ware, look for pieces in shiny metallic and sleek white. Pieces like this are very elegant—fitting for a royal celebration.

Create the Bluebird Backdrop for the table, the "At Midnight I Turn into a . . ." Party Board, and the pillow for Cinderella's glass slipper. You can also create the Pumpkin Carriage Punch Bowl. This craft takes a simple pumpkin-shaped bowl and turns it into a magical carriage with a little vinyl and a few other decorative touches. It's almost as easy as waving your wand and saying "Bibbidi-Bobbidi-Boo!"

We love finding fun ways to reference movie characters throughout our party decor. For this party, we recommend adding a strand of beads and ribbon printed to look like a measuring tape to your table. These cute props are inspired by the strand of pearls and measuring tape that Cinderella's animal friends use to create her dress.

TWO DAYS BEFORE:

Purchase all the food you need for your menu. Be sure to chill all your drink ingredients so they will be nice and cold on the day of the event. This is also a good time to make the Sparkling Gelatin Squares. These are best chilled overnight or longer, plus getting them done early will save you time on party day.

ONE DAY BEFORE:

Bake the Bibbidi-Bobbidi-Blue Velvet Cupcakes today, but wait to decorate them until the day of your party. Store your undecorated baked cupcakes in an airtight container. You can also make the fondant star cupcake toppers and frosting so that all the decorating components are ready for the next day. Make sure to store the frosting in an airtight container so that it stays soft until you are ready to use it.

THE DAY OF:

Start the day by decorating your cupcakes. Once they are iced and decorated, they will be fine sitting out on your platter until your party tonight. Cut your gelatin dessert into squares, and place them in glass stemware for serving. Store these in the refrigerator until party time.

Set up your table and your Bluebird Backdrop. Start your table by layering your gold sequin tablecloth on top of a white tablecloth. The white tablecloth underneath will provide a nice cover to the table you are using. Add a clock to the backdrop. We hung ours using clear string and a nail in the wall above the backdrop.

Spend some time getting glam for your party! Don't let the "hostess heat" rob you of your chance to look your best. Once you have everything set up, take time to dress up and get ready. The menu for this party is simple, and all that is left to do is to assemble your appetizers about forty-five minutes before your guests arrive.

Don't forget your signature drink! Pour your chilled ingredients into your pumpkin carriage bowl and set on the table, along with champagne flutes for the guests to serve themselves. For an extra touch, place rock candy swizzle sticks in your flutes.

Happy New Year!

The Lion King
"Welcome to the Pride" Baby Shower

The Lion King
"Welcome to the Pride" Baby Shower

EVENT OVERVIEW

FOR THE MENU

- Simba's Charcuterie Boards
- Lioness Quiches
- Pumba and Timon's "Rare Delicacies" Salad Cups
- Rafiki's Melon Salad
- "Slimy, Yet Satisfying" Dirt Cups
- Hakuna Matata Punch

FOR THE SPACE

- Jungle Balloon Garland
- Hakuna Matata Poster Backdrop

FOR FUN

- Animal-Cracker Favor Boxes

The Lion King opens with a brilliant sunrise over the African savanna as the animals, birds, and insects of the Pride Lands gather to celebrate the birth of Simba, their future king. While not every home is as grand as Pride Rock, and not every baby is destined to be king, every birth is cause to celebrate. After all, it's the circle of life!

With a new cub on the way, what better way to say "welcome to the pride" than with a *Lion King*–themed baby shower? This shower features a variety of menu options for both the lions (meat eaters) and the grazers (vegetarians) in your life. The decor is inspired by the African jungle and savanna, and the animal-cracker favor boxes are a sweet treat that will make your guests roar. Enjoy, party animals!

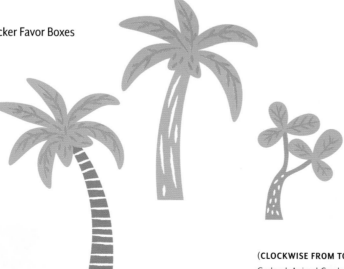

(**CLOCKWISE FROM TOP LEFT**) Hakuna Matata Punch; Jungle Balloon Garland; Animal-Cracker Favor Boxes; watering hole drink dispenser; Rafiki's Melon Salad; Lioness Quiches

SIMBA'S CHARCUTERIE BOARDS

- **Various meats, such as prosciutto and salami**
- **Various cheeses, such as Brie, Havarti, dill, and white cheddar**
- **Various fruits, such as blackberries, fresh figs, and grapes**
- **Various crackers, such as water crackers and rosemary-thyme flatbread**
- **Mini cinnamon rolls (store-bought)**

1. Arrange a variety of meats, cheeses, fruits, and crackers on small cutting boards or small plates to create individual charcuterie boards. Add a sweet touch with mini cinnamon rolls.

2. Set one charcuterie board at each place setting before the party begins.

NOTE: Please be advised that it is not recommended for pregnant women to eat cured meats or unpasteurized cheeses, so this dish is purely for the guests to enjoy.

LIONESS QUICHES

YIELD: 6 SERVINGS

- **Cooking spray for greasing**
- **6 eggs, beaten**
- **2 cups half-and-half**
- **¼ cup sliced green onions**
- **1 cup cooked diced ham**
- **1 cup shredded mozzarella cheese**
- **½ cup shredded Swiss cheese**
- **2 cups fresh spinach, lightly packed**
- **¼ teaspoon salt**
- **⅛ teaspoon pepper**
- **Dash ground nutmeg**

1. Preheat oven to 325°F. Coat six ramekin dishes with cooking spray and set aside.

2. Combine all other ingredients in bowl and mix. Divide mixture evenly between ramekins.

3. Bake in oven 30 to 35 minutes or until eggs have set. Let stand for 10 minutes before serving.

PUMBA AND TIMON'S "RARE DELICACIES" SALAD CUPS

YIELD: 8 SERVINGS

ORANGE VINAIGRETTE:

- 2 tablespoons extra-virgin olive oil
- 3 tablespoons orange juice
- 1 tablespoon Dijon mustard
- 1 tablespoon honey
- 1 tablespoon apple cider vinegar
- 1 clove garlic, minced
- ½ teaspoon orange zest
- Dash of salt
- Freshly ground black pepper

SALAD:

- 6 cups spring green lettuce mix, lightly packed
- 1 cup shelled edamame
- Endive lettuce leaves for garnishing
- Microgreens for garnishing
- Fresh mint for garnishing
- 1 orange, thinly sliced for garnishing

TO MAKE THE DRESSING:

1. Combine all dressing ingredients in a jar, attach lid, and shake until blended. Prepare dressing at least a few hours ahead of time to allow flavors to meld together.

TO MAKE THE SALAD:

1. Toss spring green lettuce mix with edamame, and fill each salad cup with mixture.
2. Garnish each salad cup with one endive lettuce leaf, microgreens, mint, and one orange slice. Serve with dressing on the side.

RAFIKI'S MELON SALAD

YIELD: 8 SERVINGS

DRESSING:

- 1 teaspoon Dijon mustard
- 1 tablespoon honey
- ¼ to ⅓ cup balsamic vinegar
- ¼ to ⅓ cup extra-virgin olive oil
- 1 clove garlic, minced
- ⅛ teaspoon salt
- ⅛ teaspoon pepper

SALAD:

- 1 large cantaloupe, diced
- ½ cup chopped fresh basil

TO MAKE THE DRESSING:

Combine all dressing ingredients in a jar and shake well to combine. Prepare dressing ahead of time to allow flavors to meld together.

TO MAKE THE SALAD:

In a large bowl, combine cantaloupe, basil, and dressing. Serve in small jars to create individual portions.

"SLIMY, YET SATISFYING" DIRT CUPS

YIELD: 8 SERVINGS

- One 14.3-ounce package chocolate sandwich cookies with crème filling
- 2 cups milk
- One 3.4-ounce package instant chocolate pudding mix
- One 12-ounce container frozen whipped topping, thawed
- Candy gummy worms for garnishing

1. Use a food processor to grind sandwich cookies until very fine. Set aside.

2. In a separate bowl, mix milk and pudding together using a spoon. Fold in whipped topping and stir well to combine.

3. Layer cookies and pudding mixture in individual jars, repeating layers until full.

4. Chill until ready to serve. Add candy gummy worms right before serving.

HAKUNA MATATA PUNCH

- 1 part peach juice
- 1 part orange juice
- 1 part mango juice
- 2 parts club soda
- Splash of cranberry juice (1 per beverage)
- Fresh mango slice for garnishing (1 per beverage)

1. Combine peach juice, orange juice, mango juice, and club soda in large drink dispenser.

2. To serve, pour individual drinks over ice and add splash of cranberry juice to each. Garnish each with fresh mango slice.

JUNGLE BALLOON GARLAND

- **Artificial tropical-leaf garland from local craft or home-goods store**
- **Balloons in gold, white, lime green, dark green, peach, and coral, in various sizes**
- **Clear string**
- **Artificial fern stems**

1. Attach inflated balloons to tropical-leaf garland using clear string. The tropical leaves should peek out in between balloons along the length of the garland.
2. Add in fern stems for additional texture. Tie these to the garland with clear string.
3. Hang over the serving table or use as a backdrop for your drink table.

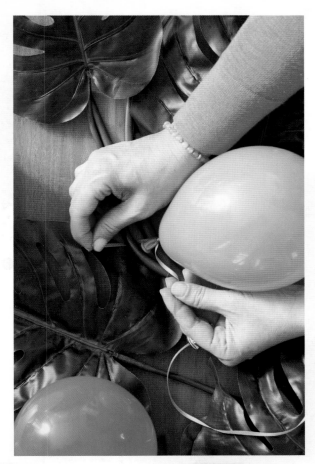

HAKUNA MATATA POSTER BACKDROP

- **Hakuna Matata Poster**
- **Foam core board**
- **Spray glue**
- **Frame (optional)**

1. Download the Hakuna Matata Poster from our online resources and print.

2. Attach the poster to the foam core board with spray glue. Frame the poster if you want, or hang it as it is.

3. Hang under the balloon garland to create your backdrop.

ANIMAL-CRACKER FAVOR BOXES

Make one for each guest, plus a few extra, just in case!

- **Clear individual-size cupcake boxes**
- **Party-paper shred**
- **Animal-cracker cookies**
- **Ribbon**

1. Fill clear cupcake boxes with a layer of party-paper shred and top with animal-cracker cookies. Be sure to put the lions on top.

2. Tie ribbon around each box and give as favors to your guests.

Putting It All Together

TWO OR MORE WEEKS BEFORE:

Coordinate a date with the mommy-to-be, get her guest list, and send out invitations so the guests know to mark their calendars for this special day.

Purchase all the craft supplies and decor items. Flowers for the expectant mother are a nice touch for this party. If you want to go the extra mile and get a special arrangement, place an order with your local florist now. For a more budget-friendly option, you can go to your local grocery store two days ahead of the party—or pick from your own garden!

ONE WEEK BEFORE:

Gather your tableware. When selecting your tableware, consider using items made of copper, wood, or other natural materials, keeping in mind the colors of the African desert. Think outside the tablecloth and use a thin throw blanket with a fringed edge to cover the table. Layered place settings could include white chargers, wooden plates, napkins in a tribal print, and small charcuterie boards. For drinkware, copper mugs are a lovely choice to add a little sophistication.

Create the Hakuna Matata Poster Backdrop and choose the shape and placement of the Jungle Balloon Garland, but wait to add the balloons until closer to your party date. No saggy balloons on party day!

TWO DAYS BEFORE:

Purchase all the food you need for your menu. Be sure to chill all your drink ingredients so they will be nice and cold on the day of the event.

Craft the balloon garland. To save time—and breath—on this craft, we recommend using a balloon pump to blow up the balloons (there's no need to use helium as the balloons will be tied to the garland). Once your garland is complete, hang it on the wall. This is a simple craft, but it is good to have time to fuss over the placement and look of the garland before you get busy preparing the final details for your party. You can also make the party favors now and have them ready to display.

ONE DAY BEFORE:

Preparing some of your menu the day before will leave you more time to set up and decorate on the day of your party. Cut up the fruit and make the dressing for Rafiki's Melon Salad so it will be ready to assemble the morning of the party. Make the dressing for the "Rare Delicacies" Salad Cups. Prepare the Lioness Quiches, but wait to bake them until the day of the party so they will be nice and warm when your guests eat them. You can also prepare the ingredients for the "Slimy, Yet Satisfying" Dirt Cups, but wait to assemble them in your jars until the day of the party.

THE DAY OF:

Start the day by setting up the tables for your party. Your garland is already hanging. Add the poster backdrop, and set up the watering hole and the favors on a small table under the backdrop. Decorate your main table with your tablecloth, floral arrangement, and place settings.

Next, it's time to start the food prep. Assemble the desserts and leave them to chill in the refrigerator until party time. Make the melon salad, portion it out into small jars for serving, and refrigerate until the party starts. Just before your guests arrive, add a small sprig of fresh basil to each cup for presentation.

Approximately ninety minutes before your party begins, bake the quiches. They will take about forty-five minutes to bake and should cool slightly before serving. While the quiches are baking, assemble Simba's Charcuterie Boards. Place one at each seat for your guests to enjoy as they come to the table.

The final food item to assemble is the salad. This is best done last so the lettuce and herbs stay fresh.

Finally, create your Hakuna Matata Punch. Pour your chilled ingredients into a large pitcher, and have your ice or frozen fruit on hand to add when your guests arrive. Party time!

Alice in Wonderland
Queen of Hearts Valentine's Day Garden Party

Alice in Wonderland
Queen of Hearts Valentine's Day Garden Party

EVENT OVERVIEW

FOR THE MENU

· The Queen's Tea Sandwiches
· Crowned Heart Sandwich Cookies
· Rose Strawberries
· Wonderland Royal Punch

FOR THE SPACE

· Queen of Hearts Plates
· Paintbrush Place Cards
· Rose Napkins
· Tea Sandwich Teacup Serving Stand

FOR FUN

· Royal Croquet Court

In one memorable scene from the 1951 animated classic *Alice in Wonderland*, Alice finds herself in the garden hedge maze, where she discovers some playing cards painting white roses red. Suddenly, the White Rabbit appears announcing the arrival of the Queen of Hearts. Nonsense ensues, and Alice finds herself facing off against the Queen in a ridiculous game of croquet.

This Valentine's Day, gather all your nonsensical friends and host a Queen of Hearts Valentine's Day Garden Party in your garden or backyard. Serve a delicious selection of tea sandwiches, heart-shaped cookies, and strawberries shaped like the lush red roses the Queen loves. Roses are the perfect flowers for this party, complementing the white, black, and red color scheme. Other fun callouts include personalized Paintbrush Place Cards and homemade rose-trimmed napkins. As for entertainment, our DIY Royal Croquet Court should make for a lively afternoon!

With this party plan, you'll have everything you need to enjoy the holiday with your closest girlfriends.

(CLOCKWISE FROM TOP LEFT) Paintbrush Place Cards; Wonderland Royal Punch; Royal Croquet Court; Queen of Hearts Plates; Rose Strawberries; Crowned Heart Sandwich Cookies

THE QUEEN'S TEA SANDWICHES

A delicious selection of sandwiches is necessary for any good garden party. Your menu includes a nice variety, sure to please the pickiest queen.

STRAWBERRY TEA SANDWICHES

YIELD: 6 SERVINGS

- 2 tablespoons balsamic vinegar
- 1 tablespoon honey
- 8 slices whole-grain or white sandwich bread, crusts removed
- One 8-ounce package mascarpone, softened
- 1 bunch fresh basil
- One 8-ounce carton fresh strawberries, thinly sliced

1. In a small saucepan, bring the vinegar and honey to a boil, and continue boiling until syrupy, about 5 minutes.
2. Arrange 8 bread slices on a piece of parchment paper. Spread mascarpone on each slice of bread. Add a layer of basil over cheese, and top with a layer of thinly sliced strawberries.
3. Drizzle honey-balsamic syrup over strawberries, and top each sandwich with remaining slices of bread.
4. Cut sandwiches into four triangles.

CUCUMBER TEA SANDWICHES

YIELD: 12 SERVINGS

- One 6.5-ounce package cucumber-and-dill spreadable cheese, softened
- ½ cup peeled, seeded, and finely chopped cucumber
- ¼ cup minced green onions
- 24 slices whole-grain or white sandwich bread, crusts removed
- Microgreens for garnishing
- Cucumber slices for garnishing

1. In a small bowl, combine spreadable cheese, cucumber, and green onions.
2. Arrange 12 bread slices on a piece of parchment paper. Divide mixture evenly and spread on each slice of bread. Add a layer of microgreens on top of spread, and top with remaining 12 bread slices.
3. Cut each sandwich into four rectangles. Add sliced cucumbers on top for a garnish, and secure with a toothpick or cupcake topper.

Tip

Use a paper towel to pat your cucumber slices dry before adding to the sandwiches. This will keep the bread from getting soggy.

ASPARAGUS, PANCETTA, AND CREAM CHEESE TEA SANDWICHES

YIELD: 6 SERVINGS

- One 16-ounce jar pickled asparagus, drained
- ½ teaspoon olive oil
- ¼ cup chopped yellow bell pepper
- One 3-ounce package diced pancetta
- 1 cup light cream cheese, room temperature
- 2 teaspoons heavy whipping cream
- 12 slices potato bread, crusts removed

1. Drain asparagus and cut into ¼-inch pieces. Set aside.

2. Heat olive oil in a small sauté pan or skillet. Sauté bell pepper and pancetta over medium-high heat for several minutes, stirring continuously, until pancetta is heated and peppers are slightly caramelized. Remove from heat and let cool.

3. In a medium bowl, beat cream cheese and heavy cream at medium speed until smooth.

4. Fold in asparagus, bell pepper, and pancetta and stir to combine.

5. Arrange 4 slices of bread on parchment paper. Spread half of cream cheese mixture on bread slices, dividing evenly.

6. Top each sandwich with another bread slice, and spread the remaining cream cheese mixture on top of that. Finish sandwiches by adding third bread slice to the top of the stacks.

7. Cut each sandwich lengthwise into thirds, and then cut each sandwich third in half. Serve immediately.

Tip

If you can't make these right before serving, make them earlier in the day, cover with damp paper towels, place in an airtight container, and refrigerate until serving time.

DISNEY FUN FACT

The actress who voices Alice, Kathryn Beaumont, also voices another iconic Disney character: Wendy Darling from *Peter Pan*.

CROWNED HEART SANDWICH COOKIES

YIELD: 12 COOKIES

- ½ cup all-purpose flour
- Store-bought sugar-cookie dough
- Red cookie icing
- Strawberry icing for decorating
- Yellow fondant for decorating
- Edible gold luster dust for dusting

SPECIAL SUPPLIES:

- Heart cookie cutter

Tip

Using store-bought cookie dough and icing will save you time, but feel free to use your own recipes.

1. Preheat oven to 350°F.

2. Knead the flour into the sugar-cookie dough until the flour is thoroughly incorporated into the dough.

3. Roll dough onto a floured surface, and use heart cookie cutters to cut out an even number of cookies. Place hearts on parchment-lined baking sheet and freeze for 10 minutes before baking.

4. Bake for 10 to 12 minutes. Let sit a few minutes on the sheet, then transfer to a cooling rack.

5. Pour store-bought red cookie icing into a small bowl. Once the cookies have cooled completely, ice half the cookies on one side by dipping the front face of each into the red icing. Set aside to dry.

6. Fill a pastry bag with the strawberry-flavored icing. Cut an opening in the pastry bag, and pipe a layer of icing onto the back face of the remaining cookies.

7. Place one red iced heart, with the icing facing out, on top of each strawberry-icing cookie to make a sandwich. Set aside to continue drying.

8. Roll out yellow fondant, and use a sharp knife to cut out small crown shapes to fit on tops of the iced heart cookies.

9. Place all the fondant crowns on parchment paper. Using a small paintbrush, dust each crown with the edible gold luster dust.

10. To attach the crowns to the red iced hearts, add a drop of red icing to the tops of each heart, and place a fondant crown on top. Let dry completely.

ROSE STRAWBERRIES

· **Fresh strawberries**

1. Wash fresh strawberries and leave whole.
2. Take one strawberry and place leaf side down. Using a paring knife, make a row of small slits around the bottom of the berry, angling the knife toward the center and slightly downward and being careful not to slice through.
3. Use the knife to gently bend each cut outward to create "petals." Repeat the process with more rows until you reach the top of the berry.
4. When you are finished, the berry will look like a rose. Repeat for all the strawberries.

WONDERLAND ROYAL PUNCH

· **1 part citrus juice blend**
· **1 part cranberry juice**
· **Splash of club soda**
· **Strawberry sliced in half for garnishing**

Combine the juices in a large pitcher. Just before serving, add a splash of club soda to the pitcher. Set the pitcher on the table alongside a bowl of sliced strawberries to use as garnish.

Tip

Freeze fresh strawberries sliced in half vertically (to look like hearts) before the party. They will keep drinks cold without watering down the drink as they melt.

QUEEN OF HEARTS PLATES

Make one of these for each place setting at your table.

- **Crowned Heart Vinyl Template** ⬇
- **Curiouser Vinyl Template** ⬇
- **White printable vinyl**
- **Black vinyl**
- **Cutting machine or scissors**
- **White plates**

1. Download the Crowned Heart Vinyl Template and Curiouser Vinyl Template from our online resources. ⬇

2. Print the Crowned Heart on white printable vinyl. Use your cutting machine or scissors to cut out the design, and stick to center of plate.

3. Use your cutting machine or scissors to cut out the phrase "Curiouser and Curiouser!" in black vinyl. Stick to the top and bottom rims of your plate.

4. Hand-wash each finished plate before serving food.

DISNEY FUN FACT

Alice in Wonderland features fourteen original songs—more than any other Disney film!

PAINTBRUSH PLACE CARDS

- **Red craft paint**
- **Craft paintbrushes, 1 for each guest**
- **Black vinyl or black permanent marker**
- **Cutting machine (optional)**

1. Fill small plastic cup with red craft paint.

2. Submerge each paintbrush in paint, and set aside to let dry.

3. Cut out each guest's name in black vinyl and stick to the handle of a paintbrush. Alternatively, use a black permanent marker to write each name.

ROSE NAPKINS

This is a great way to embellish standard white linen napkins for your party. It is not permanent, so you can remove the trim and reuse the napkins for other parties.

- **Felt rose ribbon trim**
- **Nonpermanent fabric tape**
- **White linen napkins**

1. Fold napkin in thirds to make a narrow rectangular shape. This allows the napkin to lie under each boxwood mat and drape down the front of the table. (See page 42.)

2. Cut a length of trim slightly longer than the width of the folded napkin, allowing a small amount of trim to wrap around the back.

3. Attach trim to napkin with fabric tape.

TEA SANDWICH TEACUP
SERVING STAND

- **Small white cake stand**
- **2 sturdy teacups**
- **2 white plates in different sizes**
- **White card stock**
- **Scissors**
- **Menu Cards**
- **1 party straw**
- **Double-sided tape**
- **Mounting putty**

1. Use the small white cake stand as the base.
2. Place the larger white plate on top of the cake stand. We used a plastic charger from the local craft store.
3. Create the next layer by placing a sturdy teacup in the center of the white plate.
4. Place the smaller white plate faceup on top of the teacup, and add another teacup on top of that.

Download the *Alice in Wonderland* Menu Cards from our online resources, and print each card on card stock.

5. Use double-sided tape to stick the Tea Sandwiches card onto the party straw, and secure the straw in the center of the top teacup with mounting putty.
6. Arrange your tea sandwiches on the stand just prior to serving.

Tip

This serving stand is not glued or tied together, so it is best assembled in place and treated with care.

ROYAL CROQUET COURT

- **Croquet set**
- **Spray paint in the following colors: aqua, green, orange, purple, pink, red, yellow**
- **6 plastic flamingos**
- **Drill**
- **Spade drill bit in same size as mallet handle diameter**
- **Superglue**
- **Card Soldier Template** ⬇
- **White card stock in letter, legal, and tabloid sizes**
- **Hot glue gun**
- **Royal Croquet Court Sign** ⬇
- **Stake**

1. Drill two holes in each of the plastic flamingos, one through the top of the back and the other through the tail. (This is where the handle of the croquet mallet will go, so make sure the holes line up.)

2. Slide each flamingo onto a mallet with the head of the flamingo closest to the head of the mallet. If necessary, apply a little superglue around the holes to secure the flamingos in place.

3. Spray-paint each flamingo mallet a different color, one for each player. Let dry.

4. Spray-paint the croquet balls so each ball coordinates with each mallet. Let dry.

5. Download and print the Card Soldier Template on white card stock. Hot glue the face, hands, and feet to each card. Bend one card over each end post that came with your croquet set, and secure to the hoop using hot glue. ⬇

6. Create a course in your yard with the end posts, following the instructions that came with your croquet set.

7. Download and print the Royal Croquet Court Sign. Attach the sign to your stake using a hot glue gun. Let dry. Stake it at the beginning of the course. ⬇

8. Give each player a matching mallet and ball, and let the games begin!

Tip

Flamingo lawn ornaments are easily found at your local hardware store or online.

TWO OR MORE WEEKS BEFORE:

Send out invitations to your friends, requesting the pleasure of their company by royal command.

Purchase and gather all the supplies you will need for the crafts. If there's one project you want to get done early, it's the Royal Croquet Court. While the actual work on this craft is simple, it will take some time, so don't wait. The final product is well worth the extra time.

A professionally baked and decorated cake is a great touch if you want to add a little extra to this party. If you're planning to serve a cake, place the order now to give your baker plenty of time to create something marvelous. Because it's a small gathering, you don't need something huge, and keeping the cake on the smaller side will keep the cost down.

ONE WEEK BEFORE:

Gather your decor and serving pieces. The color palette for this party is classic red, white, and black, with touches of green as a callout to the Queen's hedge maze. Graphic black-and-white fabric provides a perfect table covering and allows the green boxwood mats, red goblets, and heart accents sprinkled throughout to really pop.

We recommend a boxwood bush with red roses as a centerpiece for your main table. Find one at your local nursery, or craft one using an artificial boxwood bush and artificial roses from your local craft store.

Create the crafts for the plates, napkins, and Paintbrush Place Cards.

TWO DAYS BEFORE:

Purchase all the food and drinks you need for your menu. Be sure to chill all your drink ingredients so they will be nice and cold on party day.

ONE DAY BEFORE:

Preparing some of your menu the day before will leave you more time to set up and decorate on the day of your party. Decorate the Crowned Heart Sandwich Cookies and let them dry. Store in an airtight container until the day of the party. You can create the Rose Strawberries and store them covered in the refrigerator overnight. Prep all the ingredients for the tea sandwiches today, but wait to assemble them until the day of your party.

THE DAY OF:

Pick up your cake! This will truly delight your guests with the whimsy it will bring to your table. Set your table and arrange your serving pieces. Assemble your Tea Sandwich Teacup Serving Stand in place—you will add the sandwiches to it later. Create each place setting by layering a napkin, a boxwood placemat, a Queen of Hearts Plate, and a Paintbrush Place Card. The paintbrushes double as a fun favor too! Set up your Royal Croquet Court and set out the flamingo mallets and croquet balls!

Assemble your tea sandwiches and store them in an airtight container in the refrigerator until twenty minutes before the party starts. You can add them to your teacup stand just before your guests arrive. Add the Rose Strawberries to a plate of grapes, and set a couple of Crowned Heart Sandwich Cookies on small stands at each place setting. For the Wonderland Royal Punch, combine the juices in a large pitcher and chill in the fridge until serving time. Just before the party starts, add the splash of seltzer to the drink, and set the pitcher out alongside a bowl of sliced strawberries or frozen strawberry hearts. Now you're all set for a delightfully mad Valentine's Day garden party!

Mickey & Minnie
"Mouse Ears" Birthday Party

Get Your Ears Here!

Mickey & Minnie
"Mouse Ears" Birthday Party

EVENT OVERVIEW

FOR THE MENU

- Mickey's Karnival Dogs
- Mickey's Bowtie Pasta Salad
- A Modern Minnie Birthday Cake
- Mouse Ears Cupcakes
- Minnie's Yoo-Hoo! Tea

FOR THE SPACE

- Mickey Mouse Centerpiece
- Mickey & Minnie Cups

FOR FUN

- Personalized Mouse Ears
- Mickey Mouse Hollywood Star of Fame Photo Booth

We couldn't make a book of Disney-themed parties without a featuring a fete inspired by the most beloved Disney character of all: Mickey Mouse. Our Mickey & Minnie party focuses on the theme of mouse ears. It starts with a personalized pair of ears for each guest to wear during the party and take home at the end of the night. Is there a better way to show your love of Disney than by donning the signature ears? We don't think so! After all, it was Walt Disney himself who said, "I only hope that we never lose sight of one thing—that it was all started by a mouse."

As a kid, you probably attended at least one Mickey Mouse or Minnie Mouse party for a friend or classmate. Well our party's a little more grown-up, starting with a classy decor palette based around vintage Mickey and Minnie hues: black, white, red, and yellow. The menu is simple and casual, although it does include a showstopping Modern Minnie Birthday Cake. You'll see her signature red bow sprinkled throughout the menu, decor, and favors.

Put on a pair of ears and say cheers to another year of life, laughter, and Disney magic!

(**CLOCKWISE FROM TOP LEFT**) Mouse Ears Cupcakes; Personalized Mouse Ears; Mickey's Karnival Dogs and Bowtie Pasta Salad; Minnie's Yoo-Hoo! Tea; Mickey Mouse Centerpiece; Mickey Mouse Hollywood Star of Fame Photo Booth props

MICKEY'S KARNIVAL DOGS

Serve corn dogs with a variety of toppings and condiments, and let your guests create their own Karnival Dogs!

Tip

Arrange bowls of toppings to look like Mickey ears in the center of your serving plate.

- **Frozen corn dogs**
- **Pimento cheese**
- **Chopped pickles**
- **Mayo**
- **Ketchup**
- **Minced garlic**
- **Charred corn**
- **Cotija cheese**
- **Chili powder**
- **Cilantro**
- **Lime juice**

1. Bake corn dogs according to package instructions.
2. Arrange topping combinations in separate bowls: one for the pimento cheese and pickles, one for the mayo, ketchup, and minced garlic, and one for the remaining ingredients.
3. Set out with serving spoons so your guests can add their favorite toppings to their corn dogs.

DISNEY FUN FACT

The first time Mickey spoke was in the 1929 short *"The Karnival Kid."* His first words were "Hot dogs!"

MICKEY'S
BOWTIE PASTA SALAD

YIELD: 12 SERVINGS

- 4 tablespoons extra-virgin olive oil
- 5 tablespoons fresh lemon juice
- 1 tablespoon honey
- 3 tablespoons whole-grain Dijon mustard
- 2 garlic cloves, minced
- 12 ounces bowtie pasta, cooked al dente
- 2 cups halved grape tomatoes
- 1½ cups chopped bell peppers
- 1½ cups crumbled feta cheese
- 1 cup chopped green onions
- Salt
- Pepper

1. Add olive oil, lemon juice, honey, mustard, and garlic to a small jar. Attach the lid and shake well to combine.

2. Add the remaining ingredients to a large bowl. Drizzle the dressing evenly over all ingredients and season to taste with salt and pepper.

3. Toss everything to coat and chill in refrigerator until ready to serve.

A MODERN MINNIE BIRTHDAY CAKE

YIELD: 12 SERVINGS

CAKE:

- 2 cups white sugar
- 1 cup butter
- 4 eggs
- 2 teaspoons vanilla extract
- 2 teaspoons raspberry extract
- 3 cups all-purpose flour
- 3½ teaspoons baking powder
- 1 cup milk
- Two 16-ounce cans vanilla frosting
- White fondant
- Black fondant

SPECIAL SUPPLIES:

- Mouse Ears Cake Topper ⬇
- Black card stock

TO MAKE THE CAKE:

1. Preheat oven to 350°F. Grease and flour three 6-inch round cake pans.

2. In a mixing bowl, cream together the sugar and butter. Beat in eggs, one at a time. Add vanilla and raspberry extracts and mix. In a separate bowl, combine flour and baking powder. Add dry ingredients to creamed mixture, mixing well. Stir in the milk until batter is smooth.

3. Pour batter into prepared pans and bake for 30 to 40 minutes. Cake is done when an inserted toothpick comes out clean. Remove from oven and let cool completely.

4. Slice a thin layer off the top of each cake to create level surfaces.

TO ASSEMBLE THE CAKE:

1. Place a spoonful of vanilla frosting in the center of your cake plate, and place one layer of the cake down. Add a large spoonful of frosting on top of the layer, and use a flat knife to spread it outward toward the edges. Add the next layer of cake on top of the first, and repeat. Repeat this process until all your layers are stacked.

2. Once your layers are stacked, apply a thick layer of icing over the sides and top, completely covering the cake. Place the iced cake in the refrigerator to cool for at 30 minutes.

3. Dust your work surface with powdered sugar and roll out your fondant into a large circle about ¼ inch thick. It should be big enough to cover the entire cake in one piece.

4. Pick up the white fondant by loosely rolling it over a rolling pin and lifting it gently from the work surface. Unroll the fondant over the cake, and smooth the fondant on the top and around the sides using your hands or a flat fondant-smoothing tool. Trim off any excess around the bottom. Set aside.

5. To create the black fondant stripes, dust your work surface with powdered sugar and roll out your fondant into a large rectangle about ¼ inch thick. The rectangle should be slightly longer than the diameter of your cake. Using a ruler as your guide, cut 1-inch strips of fondant with a pizza cutter. Rub shortening on one side of each strip, and then wrap them around your cake, starting at the bottom. The shortening will glue the strips in place.

6. Download our Mouse Ears Cake Topper, print on black card stock, and cut out. ⬇

7. Add the topper to the cake, and you are done!

Tip

Flip the final layer of your cake upside down before you place it on the cake. This will make for a perfectly flat, smooth top for your cake.

MOUSE EARS CUPCAKES

YIELD: 12 CUPCAKES

- 12 iced cupcakes, homemade or store-bought

SPECIAL SUPPLIES:

- **White card stock**
- **Mickey and Minnie Cupcake Toppers** ⬇
- **Toothpicks**
- **Red ribbon with white polka dots**
- **Hot glue gun**
- **Clear string**
- **Red cupcake liners**

1. Download Mickey and Minnie Cupcake Toppers from our online resources and print on white card stock. ⬇

2. Make Minnie Mouse bows for half of your cupcakes. Fold a 2½-inch length of ribbon into a loop. Secure ends of loop with hot glue. Pinch middle of ribbon and tie with clear string to create the bow shape. Repeat until you have six bows.

3. Hot glue paper toppers to toothpicks. Hot glue bows to half of the ears to represent Minnie Mouse. Stick toppers into iced cupcakes and enjoy!

Tip

This recipe uses store-bought cupcakes to save time on a party that already includes a complex dessert. However, feel free to substitute your favorite recipe if you prefer!

MINNIE'S YOO-HOO! TEA

YIELD: 8 SERVINGS

- 2 tablespoons honey
- 3 iced hibiscus herbal tea bags
- 3 matcha green tea bags
- Raspberries for garnishing
- Strawberries for garnishing
- Mint leaves for garnishing

1. Fill a large pot with 8 cups water and bring to a boil.

2. Once the water begins to boil, remove from heat and add honey. Stir to dissolve.

3. Add all six tea bags and let steep for 10 to 15 minutes.

4. Fill a pitcher with ice.

5. Remove the tea bags, and pour tea into ice-filled pitcher. The heat of the tea will melt the ice. Chill until ready to serve.

6. To serve, add ice to a cup and pour tea over top. Garnish with raspberries, strawberries, and mint leaves.

DISNEY FUN FACT

Written by Carl Stalling and Walt Disney in 1933, the delightful song "Minnie's Yoo-Hoo"—Mickey's salute to Minnie—has been featured in several Mickey Mouse shorts and television series and on numerous Disney albums over the years.

MICKEY MOUSE CENTERPIECE

- Black spray paint
- Two 2-inch smooth Styrofoam balls
- One 4-inch smooth Styrofoam ball
- Minnie's Bow Template ⊕
- White card stock
- Rectangular vase or container for flowers
- Glue
- Tape (optional)
- Wooden skewer
- Flowers such as red roses, carnations, tulips, greenery

Tip
Make sure your balls are smooth. Using smooth Styrofoam allows the paint to adhere more easily, leaving a clean finish.

1. Spray-paint all the Styrofoam balls black and let dry.
2. Download the Minnie's Bow Template from our online resources and print on white card stock. Cut out and attach to the side of your vase using glue or tape. ⊕
3. Once the Styrofoam balls have dried, glue the two smaller balls to top of the large ball to create Mickey Mouse's famous silhouette. Push a wooden skewer into the bottom of the large ball to create a pick that will stand up in your floral arrangement.
4. Arrange flowers in vase, and place your Mickey Mouse decorative pick in the center of the bouquet.

MICKEY & MINNIE CUPS

- Red plastic cups
- White vinyl
- Printable vinyl sheets
- Mickey and Minnie Silhouettes ⊕

1. Download the Mickey and Minnie Silhouettes and print onto printable vinyl sheets. Cut out, peel, and stick to red plastic cups. ⊕
2. Set out alongside your signature drink and enjoy!

PERSONALIZED MOUSE EARS

Make one for each guest.

- **White heat-transfer vinyl**
- **Cutting machine or scissors**
- **Mouse ears headwear**
- **Towel**
- **Iron**

1. If you are using a cutting machine, create a cut file for each party guest's name. Before cutting, mirror (flip) the design. You must cut it out backward so the names are right side up when you iron them on.

2. Use your cutting machine to cut out the names. Weed out the extra vinyl so your guests' names are printed cleanly on the carrier sheet.

3. Place each name right side up on a set of ears, with the carrier sheet still attached.

4. Lay a towel over the top of the sheet to protect your iron.

5. Use a medium-hot iron to press the vinyl firmly onto the ears for about 15 seconds.

6. Remove the towel, peel carrier sheet off, and discard. The name should adhere to the ears. Say cheers! You've got ears!

Tip

If your iron has a compartment for holding water, make sure it is totally empty before applying vinyl.

MICKEY MOUSE HOLLYWOOD STAR OF FAME PHOTO BOOTH

- Mickey Mouse Hollywood Star of Fame Photo Booth Props ⬇
- Mickey Mouse photo booth props, store-bought
- White card stock
- Scissors
- Spray glue (optional)
- White foam board (optional)
- Utility knife (optional)
- Ruler (optional)
- Backdrop of your choice
- Instant camera

1. Download the Mickey Mouse Hollywood Star of Fame Photo Booth Prop from our online resources, and print it out on white card stock. Purchase the rest of your props at your local toy or craft store, or online! ⬇

2. Cut out star. To create a sturdier prop, use spray glue to attach the star to a piece of white foam board. Cut out the foam board star using a utility knife and a ruler to help keep your edges straight.

3. Set up your backdrop in the location of your choice. You can use anything you want for a backdrop, such as a Mickey Mouse–patterned fabric or crushed red velvet drape.

4. Set out props with an instant camera so guests can take fun pictures of such a memorable occasion!

DISNEY FUN FACT

Mickey Mouse was the first cartoon character to get a star on the Hollywood Walk of Fame.

Putting It All Together

TWO OR MORE WEEKS BEFORE:

Send out invitations to your friends so they can mark their calendars for this special event. This is a casual party, and you can help keep it low-key by getting a jump on the crafts and favors early. Start by purchasing all the craft supplies. Print out and prep the photo booth props, and make your Mickey & Minnie Cups. Once the RSVPs start coming in, you can also start making the Personalized Mouse Ears. These simple party favors also serve as name tags for people who don't know each other, plus they make everyone feel silly and festive.

ONE WEEK BEFORE:

Gather decor, tableware, and serving pieces in classic Mickey and Minnie colors: red, yellow, black, and white. Create or purchase your backdrop for the photo booth and the decorative pick for your floral centerpiece. Because this is a casual gathering, plan for a food table, a drink station, and a photo booth, and leave plenty of room for mingling between the three spaces. Don't forget a clever way to display the ears!

TWO DAYS BEFORE:

Purchase all the food you need for your menu and the flowers you will use in your centerpiece. Keep your flowers in water until you are ready to create your centerpiece. Be sure to chill all your drink ingredients so they will be nice and cold on the day of the event. Bake the Modern Minnie Birthday Cake today and frost it. It can chill in the refrigerator overnight and be all set for the fondant next day.

ONE DAY BEFORE:

Preparing some of your menu the day before will leave you more time to set up and decorate the day of your party. Prepare all the topping combinations for Mickey's Karnival Dogs. Put them in the bowls you'll be serving them in, and seal them to keep in the refrigerator. Prep all the ingredients for Mickey's Bowtie Pasta Salad: Cook the pasta and refrigerate it, and mix the ingredients for the dressing. All you'll have to do the day of the party is toss everything together! Make the ribbon bows for the Mouse Ears Cupcakes so they're ready for decorating the following day. Make the Minnie's Yoo-Hoo! Tea and chill in the refrigerator overnight. Finish your menu prep by decorating your cake with your black-and-white fondant stripes.

You can also create the Mickey Mouse Centerpiece today. Just make sure there's plenty of water in the vase so the flowers stay fresh.

THE DAY OF:

Start the day by preparing your space. Decorate your food table, set up your drink station, and create your photo booth. The photo booth should be an easy setup. Simply set up your backdrop in an area that gets good natural light, and set out a small table with your photo booth props and instant camera. This is also a good place to display the personalized mouse ears for your guests to grab as they arrive. They will want to put them on and snap a pic!

Once everything's set up, you can turn your attention to the food. Decorate the cupcakes, and place them on a serving platter. Finish the pasta dish and serve in a bowl. Finally, bake the corn dogs. These are best served warm, so time this so that the dogs come out of the oven about fifteen minutes before the start of your party.

Don't forget your signature drink station! Add your Mickey & Minnie Cups, a bowl of fresh raspberries, a bowl of fresh strawberries, and a bowl of fresh mint leaves. Leave a place for your pitcher of tea to be added to the table as the first guest arrives.

Enjoy and have a happy birthday party!

The Little Mermaid
Bridal Shower Brunch

The Little Mermaid
Bridal Shower Brunch

EVENT OVERVIEW

FOR THE MENU
- Les Poissons Eggs Benedict
- Ariel's Ocean Toast
- Sand Dollar Cookies
- Mermaid Smoothie Bowls
- Ariel's Bubbly Juice Bar

FOR THE SPACE
- Shell Votive Candle Favors
- Shell Place Cards

FOR FUN
- Candy Mermaid Tails

The Little Mermaid encapsulates the mermaid fantasies of girls and women everywhere: gliding through the water with a glittering tail, discovering your true love, longing to be part of their world, and finally, living happily ever after. This bridal shower celebrates the beginning of your happily ever after (or your sister's or bestie's) with a brunch inspired by Ariel and all her friends under the sea.

The mermaid theme starts with a beautiful tablescape set off with touches of driftwood, sea glass, and mermaid-scale fabric—easy to find at your local fabric store. The color palette is soft, dreamy, and beautifully bridal, with pale pinks, fresh whites, and bright pops of one of Ariel's signature colors, turquoise. The guests will feast on mermaid toast, Les Poissons Eggs Benedict, and tropical smoothie bowls, and enjoy making their own drinks from Ariel's Bubbly Juice Bar. And what will you use to enjoy this fabulous feast? Dinglehoppers, of course!

(CLOCKWISE FROM TOP RIGHT) Les Poissons Eggs Benedict; Shell Place Cards; Sand Dollar Cookies; guests can make their own drink at Ariel's Bubbly Juice Bar; use dinglehoppers for the perfect on-theme cutlery.

Tip

Keep the sauce warm
until serving by placing
the blender container in
a pan of hot tap water.

LES POISSONS EGGS BENEDICT

YIELD: 4 SERVINGS

HOLLANDAISE:

- 3 egg yolks
- ¼ teaspoon Dijon mustard
- 1 tablespoon lemon juice
- Pinch of cayenne pepper
- ½ cup pure Irish butter

ASSEMBLY:

- 4 crab cakes, store-bought
- 4 eggs
- Salt
- Freshly ground black pepper
- Fresh arugula for garnishing

TO MAKE THE HOLLANDAISE SAUCE:

1. Combine egg yolks, mustard, lemon juice, and cayenne pepper in a small blender and cover. Pulse for a few seconds to combine and set aside.

2. Melt butter in a glass bowl in the microwave. With the blender on high, slowly pour a thin stream of butter into the egg yolk mixture. It will start to thicken immediately. Keep going until all the butter has been added. Turn the blender off and set sauce aside.

TO ASSEMBLE:

1. In a hot skillet, on medium-high heat, heat crab cakes until they're warm through and crispy.

2. Bring a small pot of water to a boil, and then reduce heat until water is just slightly simmering. Poach the eggs in water for 3 to 4 minutes each or until whites have cooked through.

3. Arrange crab cakes on serving plate, and carefully place one egg on top of each crab cake. Season eggs with a bit of salt and pepper to taste.

4. Drizzle hollandaise over the stacks, garnish with arugula and a bit more freshly cracked pepper, and serve immediately.

ARIEL'S OCEAN TOAST

- **Light cream cheese, softened**
- **A few drops green food coloring**
- **Bread for toast**
- **Edible gold leaf flakes for garnishing (optional)**

1. Divide the cream cheese in half. Mix a few drops of green food coloring into half of the cream cheese and mix. Leave the other half as is.

2. Spread plain cream cheese on each slice of toast. Spread a small amount of the colored cream cheese on top of the plain cream cheese, and swirl to create waves.

3. Set the toast out on a decorative plate, and garnish with edible gold leaf flakes.

SAND DOLLAR COOKIES

YIELD: 12 COOKIES

- 3½ cups all-purpose flour
- ½ teaspoon baking powder
- ¼ teaspoon baking soda
- 1 teaspoon cinnamon
- 1 cup sugar
- 1 cup salted butter, room temperature
- 3 eggs
- 1 teaspoon vanilla extract
- 1 teaspoon almond extract
- Cinnamon sugar for dusting
- Raw almond slices for garnishing

1. In a large bowl, mix together flour, baking powder, baking soda, and cinnamon. Set aside.

2. Using a mixer on medium speed, cream together sugar and butter until very smooth, about 1 minute.

3. Add eggs to the mix and blend on medium speed. Add vanilla and almond extracts; continue blending until well combined, about 1 minute.

4. Add the dry ingredients to wet ingredients and mix well until a dough forms, about 3 to 5 minutes.

5. Wrap dough in plastic wrap and refrigerate for at least 2 hours or as long as overnight.

6. Preheat oven to 350°F and line baking sheet with parchment paper.

7. Roll out the dough to ¼ inch thick and cut out 3-inch circles with a cookie cutter. Place on baking sheet, evenly spaced.

8. Press 5 almond slices into the center of each circle in the shape of a star. This creates your sand dollar. Dust each cookie with cinnamon sugar before popping in the oven.

9. Bake for 10 to 12 minutes or until edges are slightly brown.

10. Remove from the oven and, while cookies are hot, gently press the almonds down to make sure they stick into the dough and won't fall off once cooled.

11. Let rest on baking sheet for several minutes before transferring to wire rack to cool.

Tip

Make the dough the night before the party, to cut down on prep time the day of the event.

MERMAID SMOOTHIE BOWLS

YIELD: 4 SERVINGS

- **2 frozen bananas**
- **¼ cup frozen strawberries**
- **¼ cup frozen raspberries**
- **½ cup frozen mango**
- **1 cup milk**
- **Dragon fruit balls, frozen blueberries, and blackberries for garnishing**
- **Candy Mermaid Tails (page 86) for garnish (optional)**

1. Add bananas, strawberries, raspberries, mango, and milk to a blender and blend until smooth.

2. To serve, fill each bowl with smoothie and top with garnish of choice, such as dragon fruit, frozen blueberries, frozen blackberries, and Candy Mermaid Tails.

ARIEL'S BUBBLY
JUICE BAR

- **Sparkling grape juice**
- **Fruit juice of your choice, such as peach nectar, orange, or white grape**
- **Selection of fresh fruits, such as strawberries, pineapple, and mango, cut into bite-size pieces**
- **White chocolate candy melts**
- **Candy Mermaid Tails (page 86) for garnish (optional)**

1. Chill sparkling grape juice overnight. Fill several carafes with a selection of fruit juices. (Pictured: peach nectar, white grape, and orange.) Cut up a variety of fresh fruit and place in individual bowls.

2. Set out fruit and fruit juices at your juice bar station. Set out chilled sparkling grape juice in an ice bucket. Guests can mix their own drinks and top them off with fruit garnish. Candy Mermaid Tails (page 86) make for a fun extra!

For the Space

SHELL VOTIVE CANDLE FAVORS

Make one for each place setting at your table.

- **Variety of shells**
- **Gold leaf sheets** (optional)
- **Paintbrush** (optional)
- **Craft glue** (optional)
- **Hot glue gun**
- **Candlewicks**
- **Candle wax pellets**

1. Wash and dry shells.
2. If desired, add gold leaf to outside of each shell by brushing the shell with craft glue and then adding the leaf. Brush away any excess leaf before the glue dries.
3. Hot glue one candlewick to the bottom of the inside of each shell.
4. Melt candle wax pellets according to directions on package, and slowly pour melted wax into each shell.
5. Let wax cool completely. Trim wicks and enjoy!

Tip

You can also use a cutting machine to cut out each name in vinyl or use a paint pen to write the names on the shells by hand.

SHELL PLACE CARDS

Make one for each guest.

- **Variety of shells**
- **Vinyl**
- **Spray glue**
- **Scissors**

1. Measure the size of your shells.
2. Print out guests' names on normal copy paper in a font size that fits your shells.
3. Spray glue the front side of the printed paper with the names to the back side of a sheet of vinyl. (You should be able to see the names through the white copy paper.)
4. Use scissors to cut out each name, and apply vinyl to shell for a custom place card that doubles as a favor.

CANDY MERMAID TAILS

These mermaid tails are so easy to make, and they can be used in multiple ways, for your smoothie bowls, your signature drink, or just as a sweet treat!

- **White melting chocolate**
- **Mermaid tail silicone molds, in two sizes**
- **Edible pink luster dust for dusting (optional)**
- **Clear toothpicks (optional)**

1. Melt white chocolate candy according to package instructions.

2. Pour melted candy into silicone molds, and place in refrigerator to harden for approximately 10 minutes.

3. Once hardened, gently remove candy from mold and set aside.

4. To make these into a drink garnish, use smaller tail mold, and sink a clear toothpick into the melted chocolate at the bottom of the mold.

5. The candy will harden around the toothpick as it chills. Once hardened, remove the candy from the molds and brush with edible pink luster dust.

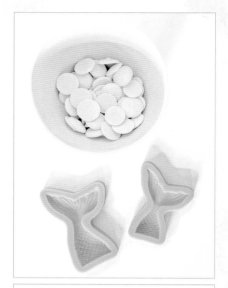

TWO OR MORE WEEKS BEFORE:

Consult with the bride-to-be, confirm her guest list, and send out invitations to this special event. Plan for your party to start at brunch hour, 11 a.m.

Purchase and gather all your supplies. It can be quite fun shopping for ocean-inspired items. If you live near the coast or have plans to travel to the coast, be sure to check local shops and markets for shells and other coastal decor. Or go on a shell-gathering expedition for an authentic touch.

Place an order for all the flowers needed for your centerpiece. You can take your clamshell bowl or vase to your local florist and they will create a lovely custom arrangement for it.

A sequin table runner in the shape of mermaid scales is a must for this party. You can order one online from any wedding supply business. Allow for a couple of weeks to ship this item so you will have it before your party.

ONE WEEK BEFORE:

Gather your decor, place settings, and serving pieces. Look for items in hues of ocean blue, turquoise, and soft coral. Create layered place settings with a soft blue dinner plate, a white shell-patterned salad plate, and a soft turquoise bowl for the Mermaid Smoothie Bowls. Don't forget your dinglehoppers! Cutlery that looks like coral on top of a soft blue napkin and a soft pink juice glass finish the setting.

A large clamshell vase is the perfect setting for a beautiful floral centerpiece, while a driftwood garland as a decor item makes a strong statement. Tuck real seashells into the arrangement and along the garland for a showstopping centerpiece any mermaid would love.

Now is a good time to do your crafts: the Shell Votive Candle Favors and the Shell Place Cards. We recommend creating a personalized place card for everyone invited in case anyone turns up who neglected to RSVP (it happens more than you'd think!). You can also make the Candy Mermaid Tails for the smoothie bowls and Ariel's Bubbly Juice Bar ahead of time. These can be stored in airtight containers in your pantry until the day of the party.

TWO DAYS BEFORE:

Purchase all the food and drinks you need for your menu. Be sure to chill all your drink ingredients so they will be nice and cold on your party day.

ONE DAY BEFORE:

Since this is an early party, getting as much done the day before the event will significantly reduce your stress the following morning. Bake the Sand Dollar Cookies and store them in an airtight container overnight. Prepare all the fruit toppings for the juice bar and store in airtight containers in the refrigerator overnight. Freeze the garnishing fruit for the smoothie bowl so it has a nice frosty look when served. You can also prepare the colored cream cheese for Ariel's Ocean Toast at this time, but you should wait to spread it on the toast until the morning of your party.

Before you go to bed, set the table and arrange your place settings and place cards. Add one shell votive favor to each place setting. Decorate the table with the floral centerpiece and driftwood garland. Add shells and any other coastal decor you have gathered.

THE DAY OF:

It's almost brunch time! You won't have a lot of time this morning, so follow this guide to get it all done before your first guest arrives. Start by making your hollandaise sauce. Keep this warm while you finish preparing the menu. Make all the smoothie bowls and put them on the table. Wait to add the fruit and mermaid tails until right before your guests arrive. Make Ariel's Ocean Toast next, and then set out the sand dollar cookies. Finish up by making Les Poissons Eggs Benedict. These should go on the table last so that they are warm when your guests arrive.

Don't forget to set up your bubbly juice bar! Set out juices in glass carafes, sparkling grape juice in an ice bucket or bottle chiller, and fresh fruit toppings in small bowls. A small cup with your Candy Mermaid Tails for garnishing finishes the station. Invite your guests to create their own bubbly drinks as they arrive.

Enjoy your day under the sea as you wish the bride-to-be a magical happily ever after!

Aladdin
Arabian Outdoor Movie Night

Aladdin
Arabian Outdoor Movie Night

EVENT OVERVIEW

FOR THE MENU

- Aladdin's Spiced and Roasted Carrots
- Princess Jasmine's Olive and Clementine Salad
- Jafar's Roasted Red Pepper Baguette with Baba Ghanoush
- The Sultan's Favorite Chicken and Olive Canapés
- Genie's Freedom Punch
- Golden Scarab Beetles

FOR THE SPACE

- Floating Candle and Floral Centerpiece
- Magic Carpet Picnic Blanket
- Tassel Pillow

FOR FUN

- Outdoor Movie
- Folding Movie Seat Backs
- Three Wishes Party Game

Magic lamps. Flying carpets. A brilliant Arabian city bursting with life and color. Who wouldn't want to escape to a world like that? This summer, when the days are long and the evenings warm, hop on your magic carpet and whisk yourself away to Agrabah and the magic of an Arabian night with this outdoor movie party inspired by *Aladdin*.

Don't let the idea of hosting an outdoor movie scare you! It's surprisingly easy to put together and a wonderful way to enjoy a summer night. This is one of the more casual parties in this book, but it's still packed with style. *Aladdin* is a visually gorgeous film, and the decor for this party honors that with some lush touches: tasseled pillows, a floating lotus centerpiece, and a Magic Carpet Picnic Blanket. Dinner is set up on a low table draped in an embroidered cloth, with a small-plates menu featuring Moroccan-inspired cuisine. Don't forget to invite the Genie! Our Three Wishes Party Game is a great way to get the conversation flowing while you wait for the sun to set and the movie to begin.

(**CLOCKWISE FROM TOP LEFT**) Floating Candle and Floral Centerpiece; Aladdin's Spiced and Roasted Carrots; Golden Scarab Beetles; Outdoor Movie; Three Wishes Party Game; Jafar's Roasted Red Pepper Baguette with Baba Ghanoush

ALADDIN'S SPICED AND ROASTED CARROTS

YIELD: 8 SERVINGS

- ¼ cup olive oil
- 1 tablespoon harissa paste
- ½ teaspoon chipotle powder
- 2 teaspoons ground coriander
- 2 teaspoons lemon juice
- 1 teaspoon honey
- 15 to 20 carrots of various sizes
- 2 tablespoons chopped fresh mint, divided
- ⅓ cup crumbled feta cheese
- Salt and pepper

1. Preheat oven to 400°F.

2. Create the marinade by whisking the olive oil, harissa paste, chipotle powder, coriander, lemon juice, and honey together in a medium bowl.

3. Slice larger carrots in half crosswise, leaving the smaller ones whole. Add the carrots to the bowl with the marinade along with half the chopped mint, and toss until carrots are nicely coated.

4. Lay the carrots out in an even layer on a lined baking sheet, and roast for 20 minutes or until tender when pierced with a fork.

5. Remove from oven and arrange on your serving plate. Sprinkle with feta cheese, remaining mint, and salt and pepper to taste. These are best served warm.

Tip
You can buy prepared baba ghanoush and roasted red peppers at your local grocery store. Check near the olive bar!

PRINCESS JASMINE'S OLIVE AND CLEMENTINE SALAD

YIELD: 8 SERVINGS

- ¼ teaspoon cumin seeds
- 1 tablespoon fresh orange juice
- 1 tablespoon white wine vinegar
- 1 tablespoon extra-virgin olive oil
- 2 clementines, peeled and chopped
- ½ yellow onion, thinly sliced
- 10 to 12 olives of your choice
- ⅛ teaspoon crushed red pepper
- ¼ cup celery leaves
- ½ cup mint leaves
- 3 radishes, cut into wedges
- Salt and pepper

1. Heat a saucepan over medium heat. Add cumin seeds and toast until slightly brown and fragrant, about 20 seconds. Let cool completely.

2. Add the orange juice, white wine vinegar, and olive oil to a jar and shake to combine.

3. Add the remaining ingredients to a bowl, drizzle the dressing over the top, and sprinkle with the toasted cumin seeds.

4. Toss everything to combine, and season with salt and pepper to taste.

JAFAR'S ROASTED RED PEPPER BAGUETTE WITH BABA GHANOUSH

YIELD: 12 SERVINGS

- 6 ounces baba ghanoush
- 6 ounces roasted red peppers in oil
- 1 baguette, sliced

1. Arrange baguette slices on a platter.

2. Layer each slice with a spoonful of baba ghanoush and a slice of roasted red pepper.

3. Drizzle a little bit of oil from the peppers on top and enjoy!

THE SULTAN'S FAVORITE CHICKEN AND OLIVE CANAPÉS

YIELD: 10 SERVINGS

- 3 tablespoons olive oil
- 1 large onion, sliced
- Salt and pepper
- 1 tablespoon minced fresh ginger
- 1 tablespoon minced fresh garlic
- 2 tablespoons garam masala
- 1 pound boneless, skinless chicken breasts
- 2 cups chicken stock
- 2 tablespoons lemon juice
- ½ cup green olives
- 20 small naan wedges
- One 8-ounce container hummus
- Fresh cilantro for garnishing

1. Heat the oil in a large skillet and sauté the onion with salt and pepper (to taste) until the onions are translucent, about 3 to 5 minutes.

2. Add ginger and garlic and continue cooking until fragrant, about one minute. Add garam marsala, mix well, and cook for another few minutes, until thoroughly combined.

3. Place chicken in the bottom of a slow cooker. Pour the onion mixture over chicken, and add chicken stock, lemon juice, olives, and salt and pepper to taste.

4. Cover and cook on high for 3 to 4 hours. Shred the chicken when done.

5. Preheat the oven to 350°F. Place naan bread slices on a baking sheet and toast for about 10 minutes. Naan should be nice and crispy but not browned.

6. Transfer naan to a serving dish, spread each slice with hummus, and add about a tablespoon of the chicken to each. Garnish with fresh cilantro and serve hot!

Tip

If you have an electric pressure cooker, this meal cooks in 15 minutes. Just sauté the ingredients in the electric pressure cooker, then add the chicken, stock, lemon juice and olives. Pressure cook for 5 minutes with a 10-minute natural release and you're ready to go!

GENIE'S FREEDOM PUNCH

YIELD: 12 SERVINGS

- **2 cups blue tropical punch**
- **1 cup limeade**
- **1 cup club soda**
- **Dry ice for effect**
- **Edible gold leaf flakes for garnishing (optional)**

1. Combine punch, limeade, and club soda in a clear pitcher.

2. Just before the guests arrive, use tongs to add a few small pieces of dry ice. (Do not use your hands; it will burn.) The pitcher will start to smoke like a genie released from his lamp!

3. To serve, pour drink into a gold-rimmed glass (don't pour any dry ice into a glass!) and add a few flakes of edible gold leaf as garnish.

Tip

Dry ice makes for a great effect, but it should not be ingested. The dry ice chips will sink to the bottom of the pitcher and should stay there until they dissipate. However, it's still best to use caution and avoid pouring any dry ice into someone's drink glass so no one gets a mouthful of dry ice by mistake!

GOLDEN SCARAB BEETLES

- **One 12-ounce package chocolate candy melts**
- **Edible gold luster dust for dusting**

SPECIAL SUPPLIES:

- **Plastic candy mold in beetle shape**

1. Melt candy melts according to package directions. Pour melted candy into candy molds.

2. Refrigerate until hardened, about 15 minutes.

3. Remove candy from molds and let sit until room temperature.

4. Brush edible gold luster dust on each beetle to make them golden in color.

Tip

If you don't have a gold bowl,
use a clear glass bowl and
spray-paint it gold!

FLOATING CANDLE AND FLORAL CENTERPIECE

- **Large gold bowl**
- **Floating candles**
- **Orchid flowers**

1. Fill large gold bowl with water and add floating candles. The number of candles you use will depend on the size of your bowl.

2. Add orchid flowers to the bowl.

3. Light the candles for a centerpiece worthy of any palace.

Tip

A gold plant stand with a white dinner plate on top makes for a simple side table to hold drinks while watching the movie. It's a nice addition to your outdoor movie setup!

MAGIC CARPET PICNIC BLANKET

- **Magic carpet throw blanket or any Arabian-themed blanket**
- **2 drapery drawback cords with gold tassels**
- **Hot glue gun**
- **Scissors**

1. Lay your magic carpet blanket down flat. If you can't find an authentic magic carpet blanket, any Arabian-themed print will do.
2. Lay the drapery cord along the long edge of the blanket with one tassel at the corner. The fringe of the tassel should hang off the corner.
3. Trim the length of your cord to fit your blanket. Once the cord is down to the correct length, cut the second tassel off the excess cord and reposition it at the end of the cord opposite the other tassel on the blanket.
4. Hot glue the cord and tassels to the blanket.
5. Repeat this process on the other side of the blanket with the second tassel cord.
6. Lay the blanket down and add some throw pillows, and you have a cozy place to watch your outdoor movie.

TASSEL PILLOW

Tassel ornaments are a quick way to turn an everyday pillow into a cushion fit for an Arabian night. You can find the tassels at most craft stores or online. Get them in a variety of colors for colorful display.

- **Throw pillow**
- **4 tassel ornaments**
- **Hot glue gun**

1. Hot glue a tassel to each corner of your pillow.
2. Set the pillow aside and allow glue to cool completely before using.

Tip

You want the area around your movie screen to be as dark as possible. The more lights that are on nearby, the more it will affect the brightness of the movie on the screen.

OUTDOOR MOVIE

- **White blackout movie-screen fabric, 66 by 110 inches, or a plain white sheet**
- **10 grommets**
- **5 bungee cords**
- **Movie projector**
- **Streaming device or DVD player**
- **Tripod, chair, or table**
- **Bluetooth speaker**

1. Decide where you want to set up your movie. It will work best in a spot that doesn't get a lot of light from windows, streetlamps, or other lights after the sun goes down.

2. Follow the grommet package instructions to add grommets to the ends of your movie-screen fabric or sheet. To give your fabric extra strength, fold the ends of fabric over before adding the grommets, creating a double layer of fabric for the grommets to hold.

3. Wrap the fabric around two trees or columns by hooking bungee cords between the grommet holes—one cord between the top grommets, one between the bottom grommets. Your bungee cords should be shorter than the distance between the columns so that they stretch, pulling the fabric taut and creating a flat screen.

4. Connect your projector to your tripod. If you don't have a tripod, you can set the projector on a chair or small table. Position the projector so it is facing the screen, and move it closer or farther away so that the image fills the screen.

5. Attach your streaming device. This is the simplest way to view the movie with minimal equipment, but you could also use a DVD player.

6. Connect your Bluetooth speaker for better sound quality. The projector does have sound, but it may not be clear or loud enough to enjoy the movie with a group of friends. Have fun!

FOLDING MOVIE SEAT BACKS

Make one for each guest.

- **2 pieces plywood, 16 by 18 inches each**
- **Spray paint, white or color of your choice**
- **2 continuous hinges**
- **2 wood boards, 1 by 2 by 18 inches**
- **Six 2½-inch wood screws**
- **Four 5-inch wood screws**
- **Drill or screwdriver**
- **Battery-operated string lights**

1. Have your local hardware store or lumberyard cut 2 pieces of plywood, each measuring 16 inches by 18 inches.

2. Spray-paint the plywood pieces white, or the color of your choice. Let dry.

3. Attach the 2 pieces of plywood by their longer ends using 2 continuous hinges and screws.

4. Attach one 1-by-2-inch board to the inside bottom edge of each piece of plywood, using 2½-inch screws.

5. Screw two 5-inch screws through the top of each 1-by-2-inch board, about one inch from each edge so the screw sticks out of the bottom of the board. These will pierce the ground and hold the plywood in place.

6. To use, open the seat backs to form a triangle, and set them on the grass or dirt in front of your movie screen. Gently press the seat backs into the ground, allowing the 5-inch screws to dig into the ground, so the seats are secure.

7. Hang a strand of battery-operated string lights across the tops of the seat backs. Add a few pillows and blankets, and enjoy the show!

DISNEY FUN FACT

The Genie's lamp can be seen on the back of treasure-hoarding crab Tamatoa in *Moana*, which, like 1992's *Aladdin*, was directed by Ron Clements and John Musker.

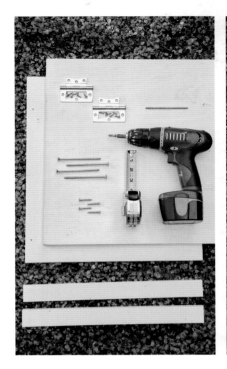
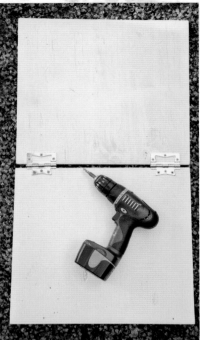
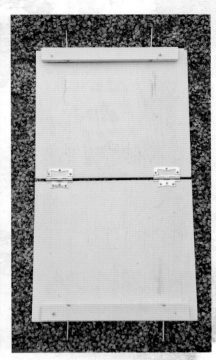

THREE WISHES PARTY GAME

This game is a fun way to pass the time while enjoying your dinner and waiting for the sun to go down to start the movie. Think you know your guests well? You might be surprised!

- **Three Wishes Party Game Cards** ⊙
- **White card stock**
- **Scissors**

1. Download our printable Three Wishes Party Game Cards from our online resources. Print and cut out enough cards for each of your guests. ⊙

2. During dinner, pass the cards out to each guest. Have everyone write down their three wishes. Encourage them to be creative and outlandish!

3. Designate a reader to share each card out loud, and try to guess whose card is whose.

Putting It All Together

TWO OR MORE WEEKS BEFORE:

Outdoor movie nights are so fun and surprisingly easy to set up. Purchase the equipment early to make sure it all works and test your setup. A plain white sheet will work for your screen, but we recommend going the extra mile and using movie-screen fabric. This special fabric is not too expensive and makes a world of difference because it prevents the light of the projector from shining through the fabric, resulting in a brighter image.

Decide where you want to hang your screen, ideally in the darkest part of your yard. The more lights nearby, the duller the image will be. Add the grommets to your movie-screen fabric and test the setup of your projector and screen. This will help you get familiar with the equipment and make day-of setup a breeze.

Now is also the time to gather your craft supplies and order the sari cloth for your table. You can find beautiful, unique authentic saris through marketplace sellers online. We recommend blue

and purple, with touches of gold—classic *Aladdin* colors. Finally, don't forget to send out invitations to your friends so they know to save the date for this unique event!

ONE WEEK BEFORE:

Gather the decor, tableware, and serving dishes for your *Aladdin*-inspired table. A low table with guests seated on cushions pays tribute to the Arab and Eastern cultures in which the story is grounded. A coffee table will work fine.

For tableware, we recommend gold-rimmed salad plates, matched with gold-rimmed glasses. Salad plates are perfect for this type of dinner, giving guests a chance to try a small portion of every dish on the menu. Light your table with lanterns and hurricane candleholders to add to the glow of the evening, and scatter gold coins to add a touch of shine and fun callout to the Forbidden Treasure of the Cave of Wonders. And don't forget your magic lamp!

Once you've got your table planned, you can dive into the crafts. Create your Tassel Pillows, Magic Carpet Picnic Blanket, and Folding Movie Seat Backs. If you're using a glass bowl for your Floating Candle and Floral Centerpiece, spray-paint it gold so it's ready for the table on the day of the party. You can also print and cut out the Three Wishes Party Game Cards. Don't forget to have enough pens on hand for everyone to play the game.

TWO DAYS BEFORE:

Purchase all the food and drinks you need for your menu, but leave off buying the dry ice until the day of the event. Purchase the orchids you will use in your centerpiece. One stem of orchids should provide enough blossoms to fill your centerpiece. Don't forget your floating candles!

Be sure to chill all your drink ingredients so they will be nice and cold on your party day.

ONE DAY BEFORE:

Preparing some of your menu the day before will leave you more time to set up and decorate on the day of your party. Since most of these menu

items are best served hot, today is more about prepping than cooking, so just chop and measure everything to the right proportions. You can fully prepare the Golden Scarab Beetles today. These can be stored overnight in a container.

THE DAY OF:

Begin the day by getting the slow cooker started for the Sultan's Favorite Chicken and Olive Canapés. The chicken will cook for three to four hours, so be sure to start it early enough. Now is also the time to buy the dry ice for your signature drink. Store the ice in a dry cooler (a Styrofoam cooler will work fine) to keep it from evaporating too quickly. Remember: Never touch dry ice with your hands. It will burn. Use tongs instead.

Set your table and create your centerpiece. Choose the platters you will be serving your dishes on and arrange the empty platters on the table. This makes it easy to add your hot dishes to each platter as they become ready. When the last dish is set out, you are ready to eat!

It's time to finish your menu. Prepare Jafar's Roasted Red Pepper Baguette with Baba Ghanoush first. Next, prepare Princess Jasmine's Olive and Clementine Salad. These two dishes are good at room temperature, and there is no cooking involved. They will stay fresh while you prepare the other items. Wait to cook the remaining items until the last hour before your guests arrive to ensure that everyone will enjoy these dishes hot.

Don't forget your signature drink! Add your punch, limeade, and club soda to a pitcher, and chill in your refrigerator. Create a drink station with glasses and a small bowl of edible gold flakes for garnishing, and place your pitcher next to the station as your first guest arrives. Drop in a few pieces of dry ice and impress your friends!

Let your Arabian Outdoor Movie Night begin!

The Princess and the Frog
New Orleans Dinner Party

The Princess and the Frog
New Orleans Dinner Party

EVENT OVERVIEW

FOR THE MENU

- Tiana's Famous Gumbo
- Ray's Cajun Shrimp Dip
- Man-Catching Beignets
- Bayou Queen Punch

FOR THE SPACE

- Ray's Firefly Friends

FOR FUN

- New Orleans Jazz Playlist
- Tiana's Beignet Mix Favors
- Golden Mirror Signboard
- Roaring Twenties Selfie Station

S et in New Orleans, *The Princess and the Frog* tells the story of Tiana, a girl whose dreams of opening her own restaurant take a slight detour when she kisses a frog and turns into one herself. Tiana and Naveen hop through a golden, jazz-soaked New Orleans decked out in its 1920s best, encountering sinister witch doctors, horn-playing alligators, Cajun fireflies, and bayou-dwelling voodoo queens along the way. In the end, they both get their wishes, proving once and for all that "dreams do come true in New Orleans."

When dreams come true, it means just one thing: party time! Celebrate a big accomplishment or a new chapter in your life with a 1920s New Orleans–style dinner party inspired by Tiana's heartwarming story. The menu takes center stage in this party—Tiana is a chef, after all. Her famous gumbo, Man-Catching Beignets, and Cajun shrimp dip inspired by Ray the firefly will have guests begging for seconds. Set the ambience with a little New Orleans jazz, and capture your memories with an instant camera and a collection of zany 1920s photo props. We hope you enjoy your trip to the Big Easy!

(**CLOCKWISE FROM TOP LEFT**) Man-Catching Beignets; decorate chairs with sashes, feathers, and Mardi Gras beads; Tiana's Famous Gumbo; Roaring Twenties Selfie Station; lotus flowers are a nice decorative touch; Ray's Firefly Friends

TIANA'S FAMOUS GUMBO

YIELD: 12 SERVINGS

- 1 rotisserie chicken, diced and shredded
- ¼ cup vegetable oil
- 1 pound kielbasa sausage, cut into pieces
- ½ cup all-purpose flour
- ¼ teaspoon salt
- ¼ teaspoon pepper
- 5 tablespoons salted butter, divided
- 1 large yellow onion, chopped
- 6 cloves garlic, minced
- 1 large green bell pepper, seeded and chopped

- 1 cup celery, chopped
- ¼ cup Worcestershire sauce
- 4 cups chicken broth
- 2 teaspoons chicken bouillon
- 2 cups diced fresh tomatoes
- 2 cups chopped fresh okra (about 16 pods)
- 5 green onions, sliced, plus more for garnishing
- ½ pound small shrimp
- 2 tablespoons Tabasco sauce
- 6 cups cooked white rice

1. Cut and shred the rotisserie chicken and set aside.
2. In a large stockpot, heat oil over medium-high heat. Add the sliced sausage and cook until browned, about 5 to 8 minutes.
3. Remove sausages, and add flour, salt, pepper, and 2 tablespoons of the butter to the oil. Stir continuously over medium-high heat until brown.
4. Reduce heat to low, and stir in the remaining butter, onion, garlic, bell pepper, and celery. Cook this mixture for 10 minutes or until the vegetables are tender.
5. Stir in the Worcestershire sauce, and add more salt and pepper to taste. Continue stirring while mixture cooks on low for about 10 more minutes.
6. Add chicken broth, bouillon, shredded chicken, and cooked sausages, and stir. Turn the heat up to medium to bring the gumbo to a boil.
7. Reduce the heat and cover. Simmer for 45 minutes, stirring occasionally.
8. Stir in the tomatoes and okra. Cover again and simmer for another hour, stirring occasionally.
9. Take the gumbo off the stove and stir in the green onions, shrimp, and Tabasco sauce.
10. Serve over cooked white rice and garnish with fresh chopped green onion. Enjoy!

RAY'S CAJUN SHRIMP DIP

YIELD: 12 SERVINGS

- **One 12-ounce package frozen small salad shrimp, defrosted**
- **2 to 3 green onions, sliced**
- **1 red bell pepper, diced**
- **¼ cup sour cream**
- **1 cup light cream cheese**
- **¼ cup parmesan cheese**
- **1 cup shredded cheddar cheese**
- **1 tablespoon lemon juice**
- **Zest of 1 lemon**
- **1 tablespoon Cajun seasoning**
- **2 teaspoons Worcestershire sauce**
- **Crackers or baguette slices for serving**

1. Preheat the oven to 375°F and prepare a baking dish by lightly greasing the sides and bottom.

2. Combine all ingredients except the crackers or bread in a large bowl and mix well. Pour the mixture into the prepared baking dish.

3. Bake for 18 to 20 minutes or until the mixture is slightly bubbly. Serve with crackers or baguette slices. Enjoy warm!

MAN-CATCHING BEIGNETS

YIELD: 12 SERVINGS

- 1½ cups warm water
- ½ cup white sugar
- 2¼ teaspoons active dry yeast
- 2 large eggs
- 1 cup evaporated milk
- 1 teaspoon vanilla extract
- 1 teaspoon salt
- 6½ cups bread flour, divided
- ¼ cup unsalted butter, softened
- 1 quart vegetable oil for frying
- ¼ cup confectioners' sugar

1. Stir together the warm water, sugar, and yeast in a large mixing bowl. Let sit and dissolve for 5 to 10 minutes, until smooth.

2. Add the eggs, evaporated milk, vanilla extract, and salt, and mix on low with a hand mixer until combined.

3. Add 3 cups of the flour, one cup at a time. Add the butter and continue to mix on low until dough is sticky but smooth. Add the remaining flour and mix until just combined.

4. Cover with plastic wrap and chill overnight. The dough will rise as it chills.

5. Remove dough from refrigerator and let rest at room temperature for about 30 minutes.

6. Roll out the dough on a floured surface to ⅛ inch thick, and slice into 2-inch squares.

7. Heat vegetable oil in a Dutch oven or electric fryer until the temperature reaches 375°F.

8. Place a few of the uncooked beignets in the hot oil and fry them, turning once, until they are puffy and golden brown on both sides, about 1 to 2 minutes per side. Remove the beignets from the oil and drain on paper towels.

9. Transfer the beignets to a serving dish and dust with a light layer of powdered sugar. Repeat with remaining dough squares. Once all the beignets are done, add a generous dusting of powdered sugar on top of the pile and serve.

BAYOU QUEEN PUNCH

- 1 part white grape juice
- 1 part ginger juice
- Fresh cucumber slices, for garnishing

1. Muddle cucumber, white grape juice, and ginger juice in a cocktail shaker.

2. Add ice and shake.

3. Strain and pour into glass. Garnish with fresh cucumber slice.

DISNEY FUN FACT

Tiana is the only Disney Princess with a job. Though other heroines like Cinderella and Mulan were no strangers to hard work, Tiana is the only princess who is paid for her efforts.

RAY'S FIREFLY FRIENDS

- **Glass terrariums**
- **Moss**
- **Battery-operated lights**

1. Place battery-operated lights in a glass terrarium.
2. Fill the jar with moss, but not too tightly. Make sure the lights are able to peek through.

DISNEY FUN FACT

The star that Ray calls his Evangeline is actually the planet Venus, named after the Roman goddess of love.

For Fun

NEW ORLEANS JAZZ PLAYLIST

Set the mood for the evening with a playlist of classic New Orleans jazz music!

PLAYLIST

1. "When the Saints," Louis Armstrong
2. "Drop Me Off in New Orleans," Kermit Ruffins
3. "It's Been So Long," Edmond Hall
4. "Almost There," *The Princess and The Frog* Soundtrack
5. "Second Line (Joe Avery's Blues)," Wynton Marsalis Quintet
6. "Yes Sir! That's My Baby," Firehouse Five Plus Two
7. "Dig a Little Deeper," *The Princess and The Frog* Soundtrack
8. "Perdido Street Blues," Louis Armstrong
9. "Creole Jazz," Dutch Swing College Band
10. "Down in New Orleans," *The Princess and The Frog* Soundtrack

TIANA'S BEIGNET MIX FAVORS

- Tiana's Famous Beignets Jar Label ⬇
- 1 sheet label paper
- Scissors
- Store-bought beignet mix
- 12 half-pint mason jars

1. Download Tiana's Famous Beignets Jar Label and print as many as you need on label paper. Trim labels with scissors. ⬇
2. Add 1 cup of store-bought beignet mix to each mason jar.
3. Screw lids onto jars and apply labels to the lids and sides.
4. Set out the jars for guests to take home at the end of the party.

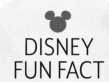

GOLDEN MIRROR SIGNBOARD

This can be used as part of your selfie station or for general decor, depending on the message!

- **Large framed mirror**
- **Gold spray paint**
- **White paint pen**

1. Find a large framed mirror, the more ornate the better. Remove the mirror glass, if possible. If you cannot remove the glass, cover it with kraft paper. Either tape it to secure the paper in place, or tuck the paper under the frame edge to cover the mirror.

2. Spray-paint the frame of the mirror gold, and let dry completely. Once dry, replace the glass in the frame or remove the kraft paper.

3. Use a white paint pen to handwrite your message on the mirror. Don't worry about it being perfect!

Tip

Don't worry about spending a ton of money on this—the mirror will look very elegant and fancy once it's painted. Check your local thrift store to find a great deal.

ROARING TWENTIES SELFIE STATION

- **Golden Mirror Signboard (instructions above; optional for this craft)**
- **Easel**
- **Art deco fabric backdrop**
- **Roaring Twenties props**
- **Kissing frog figurine**
- **Instant camera (optional)**

1. Order a set of photo props in the Roaring Twenties style and a kissing frog figurine. Have fun with your props. You can include some Mardis Gras masks, feather boas, and more.

2. Hang art deco fabric for your backdrop, and set up your Golden Mirror Signboard on an easel.

3. Set out props, kissing frog, and instant camera and get ready for a fun night of picture-taking!

DREAMS DO COME TRUE

Tip

If you don't have an instant camera, encourage guests to use their phones. It is a selfie station, after all!

Putting It All Together

TWO OR MORE WEEKS BEFORE:

A big accomplishment is best celebrated with friends and family. Send out invitations now to give your guests a heads-up about this special evening. Purchase the supplies you will need for your crafts, and order the props for your Roaring Twenties Selfie Station. We recommend an instant camera for this activity. It's a novel touch that feels a bit vintage and makes taking photos much more fun. Plus, guests can take home their photos at the end of the evening as a nice keepsake from a special occasion.

ONE WEEK BEFORE:

Prepare the crafts, gather your tableware and room decor, and plan out your place settings. When planning your table, let Tiana's Palace be your inspiration. Cover your tables with emerald-green tablecloths, and dress up your chairs with white chair sashes, ostrich feathers, and pearl beads. Add touches of rose gold and copper throughout the party to bring in a little New Orleans elegance. Don't forget your kissing frog!

TWO DAYS BEFORE:

Purchase all the food and drinks you need for your menu. Be sure to chill all your drink ingredients so they will be nice and cold on the day of the party. Download the songs for the New Orleans Jazz Playlist, and make sure your speakers are set up to enjoy classic Dixieland jazz through the night. Have fun adding to the playlist and discovering more of this fun and upbeat music.

ONE DAY BEFORE:

Preparing some of your menu the day before will leave you more time to set up and decorate the day of your party. Prepare and cook Tiana's Famous Gumbo. This dish is better the second day because the flavors have time to really meld together. You can also prepare Ray's Cajun Shrimp Dip, but wait to bake it until the day of your party so it's nice and hot when served; just store it covered in your refrigerator tonight. Prepare the dough for your Man-Catching Beignets. This dough will need to rise overnight.

THE DAY OF:

Set your table and arrange your selfie station. Be sure your kissing frog is front and center—he will be the highlight of the party! For the table, start with an emerald-green tablecloth or fabric. Create each place setting by layering a vintage charger with ornate accents, plates with rose-gold touches, and a beautiful green napkin. Add your cutlery and glasses, and top each setting with a copper mug for the gumbo. Add the terrariums to the table, and accent with lotus flowers, lily pads, and small votive candles to create a gentle ambient light. Don't forget to add your decorated chairs!

For your selfie station, start by hanging a rose-gold, art deco–inspired fabric in your chosen spot.

An upholstered bench is optional, but it's a nice touch as it gives guests a big prop to pose on. Set up your easel with the mirror sign and a few balloons to encourage your friends to come have fun in the selfie station!

Finish cooking your beignets, and bake your shrimp dip. Don't forget your signature drink! Add the juices to a pitcher, along with a few fresh cucumber slices. Let it chill in your refrigerator until party time. Create a drink station with glasses and a bowl of cucumber slices for garnishing. Add the pitcher just as the first guest arrives.

Enjoy!

Moana
Motunui Island Summer Barbecue

Moana
Motunui Island Summer Barbecue

EVENT OVERVIEW

FOR THE MENU

- Motunui Sliders
- Chief Tui's Classic Chicken Kebabs
- Tamatoa's Shiny Pineapple Bites
- HeiHei's Cheese and Melon Bites
- Te Fiti's Tropical Punch

FOR THE SPACE

- Kakamora Coconuts
- Tropical Leaf Place Cards

FOR FUN

- DIY Flower Lei Favors

Moana is a story of the daughter of an island chief who has a special connection to the ocean. She sets sail on a dangerous mission to find the shape-shifting demigod Maui, hoping he can restore the stolen heart of the goddess Te Fiti and save Moana's home and people.

Fire up the grill and bring a taste of Motunui to your summer barbecue with chicken kebabs, pork sliders, and chocolate-dipped pineapple bites. We recommend hosting this party outside, preferably at the beach or the lake to really set the island mood. A backyard pool also works! Add a tropical flower centerpiece, Te Fiti–inspired leaf place cards, and Kakamora-crafted coconut cups, and you've got a barbecue fit for a demigod. What can we say, except . . . you're welcome!

(CLOCKWISE FROM TOP LEFT) Kakamora Coconuts; Motunui Sliders; seashells add a nice touch to your table; Tropical Leaf Place Cards; Tamatoa's Shiny Pineapple Bites; DIY Flower Lei Favors

MOTUNUI SLIDERS

YIELD: 12 SERVINGS

- 2 teaspoons salt
- 2 teaspoons pepper
- 2 teaspoons garlic powder
- 1½ pounds pork tenderloin
- ⅔ cup brown sugar barbecue sauce
- One 8-ounce can pineapple slices, drained (reserve juice)
- One 12-ounce package Hawaiian dinner rolls
- Grilling spray
- One head of lettuce
- Pepper jack cheese, sliced
- 6 strips cooked bacon

1. Heat broiler with rack in top position.
2. Combine salt, pepper, and garlic powder to create a dry rub. Rub generously on all sides of pork tenderloin. Place on rimmed baking sheet lined with foil.
3. Broil 10 to 12 minutes, until internal temperature reaches 145°F. Let rest for 10 minutes.
4. Slice pork into 1-inch slices. Preheat grill on medium heat.
5. In a small bowl, stir together barbecue sauce and 2 tablespoons of pineapple juice. Brush barbeque sauce mixture on each side of tenderloin slices.
6. Grill 3 to 4 minutes on each cut side or until sauce thickens and grill marks are visible.
7. Slice dinner rolls in half, spray cut sides with grilling spray, and toast on grill to desired doneness.
8. Brush each side of the pineapple slices with sauce and grill for 2 to 4 minutes (turning once) or until grill marks are visible. Remove from grill and cut into thirds.
9. Assemble sliders by spreading the remaining barbecue sauce mixture on the bottom halves of the rolls, then layering a piece of lettuce, slice of pork, cheese, bacon, and pineapple. Finish with top half of rolls and serve.

DISNEY FUN FACT

"Moana" is both a name and a word in many Polynesian languages. It means "ocean."

CHIEF TUI'S CLASSIC CHICKEN KEBABS

YIELD: 12 SERVINGS

MARINADE:

- 1 cup soy sauce
- ½ cup apple cider vinegar
- ½ cup honey
- ¼ cup diced onion
- 2 tablespoons vegetable oil
- 4 cloves garlic, minced
- 1 teaspoon ground ginger
- Salt and pepper

KEBABS:

- 1¾ pounds boneless, skinless chicken breast, chopped into 1¼-inch cubes
- 3 heaping cups fresh cubed pineapple (about ¾ of a 3-pound pineapple)
- 1½ large green peppers, cut into bite-size pieces
- 1 large red onion, cut into bite-size pieces

TO MAKE THE MARINADE:

Add all marinade ingredients to a small bowl and whisk thoroughly to combine.

TO MAKE THE KEBABS:

1. Pierce chicken with a fork and place in a gallon-size freezer bag.
2. Pour marinade into the bag and seal.
3. Place the bag in the refrigerator and allow chicken to marinate for at least a few hours, ideally overnight.
4. Heat grill to medium-high. Slide components onto a skewer, alternating pieces of chicken, pineapple, onion, and bell pepper.
5. Grill until meat is cooked and veggies tender, about 8 to 10 minutes.

TAMATOA'S
SHINY PINEAPPLE BITES

YIELD: 8 SERVINGS

- **One 12-ounce package white melting candy wafers**
- **1 fresh pineapple, peeled and cored**
- **Chocolate melting wafers**
- **Various gold sprinkles for decorating**
- **Edible gold luster dust for dusting**

SPECIAL SUPPLIES:

- **Silicone mini seashell molds**

1. Melt white candy wafers according to package instructions and pour into mini seashell silicone molds.

2. Place in freezer for 5 to 10 minutes to harden. Remove candy seashells from silicone molds and set aside.

3. Slice pineapple into large circles.

4. Melt chocolate wafers according to package instructions. Pat dry one end of pineapple slice and dip into chocolate. Place dipped slice onto parchment-lined baking sheet.

5. Add a few candy seashells to the chocolate-dipped top of each pineapple slice, and add gold sprinkles. Let fruit sit on tray until chocolate hardens.

6. When the chocolate has hardened completely, dust the candies with edible gold luster dust to make everything shiny.

DISNEY FUN FACT

Maui's hook was inspired by the constellation called Maui's Fishhook, aka Scorpio.

HEIHEI'S CHEESE AND MELON BITES

YIELD: 12 SERVINGS

- ¼ cup honey
- ¼ cup lemon juice
- 1 melon, such as honeydew, cantaloupe, or mini seedless watermelon, sliced
- ¼ cup mint, minced, plus extra for garnishing
- One 5.2-ounce container garlic-and-herb soft, spreadable cheese
- One 6-ounce package blackberries
- One 6-ounce package blueberries

1. Add honey and lemon juice to a small jar and shake until well combined.

2. Place melon and ¼ cup of minced mint in a bowl. Pour dressing on top and toss until melon is coated.

3. Lay melon slices out on a serving dish of your choice. Spread a small amount of cheese on each slice and top with blackberries, blueberries, and a single mint leaf for garnishing.

TE FITI'S TROPICAL PUNCH

YIELD: 12 SERVINGS

- 3 cups blue tropical punch
- 1 cup pineapple juice
- 1 cup orange juice
- Lime slices for garnishing

In a large pitcher, add the punch and juices. To serve, pour into a glass filled with ice. Garnish with a slice of lime.

Tip

Double the recipe
if needed to fill
your pitcher.

KAKAMORA COCONUTS

These fun coconuts make for a fun accent! Use them as decorations, small planters, cups, or favors for your guests.

- **White air-dry modeling compound**
- **Plastic coconut cups**
- **Acrylic paint in red, tan, brown, and white**
- **Mod Podge**
- **Rope twine**
- **Variety of shells**
- **Hot glue**
- **Paper straws with wood grain design (optional)**

1. Create the bones for the Kakamora headdresses by taking a small piece of modeling compound and forming it by hand into the shape of a bone. Let dry overnight. The compound will harden and become soft and sturdy when dry. Make one bone for each coconut cup.

2. Paint a Kakamora face on each coconut cup. Use tan for the background of the face, white for the mouth, brown for the eyes, and red for the details.

3. Let the cups dry completely, and then cover the entire cup with a coat of Mod Podge to protect the painted faces.

4. Wrap each bone with rope twine. Hot glue one bone and three shells to the top of each coconut. Let hot glue cool to harden.

5. If using the Kakamora Coconuts as drinking cups, add a paper party straw through the center of the lid before serving.

Tip

Make sure each paint layer is fairly dry before adding the next.

TROPICAL LEAF PLACE CARDS

Make one for each guest.

- **Artificial tropical leaves**
- **Motunui Island Shell Template**
- **Vinyl in the color of your choice**
- **Cutting machine**

1. Measure the size of your leaves to figure out the best font size for your guests' names.

2. Download the Motunui Island Shell Template from our online resources. ⬤

3. Use your cutting machine to print out each guest's name on vinyl.

4. Apply vinyl name and shell to each leaf for a custom place card.

Tip

If you don't own a cutting machine, you can print out the names and symbols on normal copy paper, attach them to the vinyl, and cut the designs out with scissors.

Tip

Print out the DIY Flower Lei Favors Instructions from our online resources so guests can reference them when creating their leis.

DIY FLOWER LEI FAVORS

Help each guest get into the island spirit with a DIY lei they can create themselves!

- **Flowers (fresh or fake)**
- **Large craft or yarn needle**
- **Waxed thread**
- **Scissors**

1. Cut the stems off the flowers just beneath the head.

2. Cut a length of waxed thread slightly longer than you'd like your lei to be. Thread it through your needle, and tie it off.

3. Carefully thread the needle through the center of each flower from the bottom to the top. Make sure to leave a few inches of spare thread at the bottom of your lei.

4. Continue stringing flowers until lei is complete. Cut the thread off at the needle, and tie off both ends.

Tip

Do not leave your craft needles out in the open. Keep them in a closed container or a pin cushion.

TWO OR MORE WEEKS BEFORE:

Send out invitations to your friends to get this party on their calendar! Purchase the supplies for the crafts, and make the Kakamora Coconuts. The coconuts are easy to make, but you do need time to wait between paint colors, so these are best done when you have plenty of time.

ONE WEEK BEFORE:

Gather your decor and your place settings. Build your decor around natural colors and finishes to bring in the island setting. Tropical leaves, woven materials, wooden napkin rings, and ocean-colored napkins help create the essence of Motunui. If possible, plan on eating outdoors. If you don't have an outdoor table, you can always set up folding tables and cover them with tablecloths.

TWO DAYS BEFORE:

Purchase all the food you need for your menu, as well as all the flowers you will need for your DIY leis and your centerpiece. Be sure to chill all your drink ingredients so they will be nice and cold on the day of your barbecue.

ONE DAY BEFORE:

Preparing some of your menu the day before will leave you more time to set up and decorate on the day of your party. Prepare and cook the pork tenderloin for the Motunui Sliders. Once you broil and slice the pork, store the slices overnight in your refrigerator. Save the grilling for the day of the party so the pork will be hot and fresh off the barbecue.

Cut the vegetables, and prepare and marinate the chicken for the kebabs. You could assemble them today as well, if the meat has marinated long enough.

THE DAY OF:

Set your table and create your floral centerpiece. Set each place by layering a charger, plate, and napkin. Top each plate with a Kakamora Coconut and a Tropical Leaf Place Card. Add your cutlery and glasses. Finish with your tropical floral centerpiece. A few shells on the table near the flowers and a strand of Hawaiian nuts is a nice extra touch.

Prepare Tamatoa's Shiny Pineapple Bites and set aside. These will stay fresh until your guests arrive and enjoy them. Prepare HeiHei's Cheese and Melon Bites. You can cut the melon, wash the berries and mint, and store ingredients in the refrigerator until you are ready to assemble and serve your appetizer. Assembly can take place fifteen minutes prior to your guests arriving to ensure optimum freshness.

If you are using fresh flowers for the leis, remove all the flowers from the stems and put them in a bowl. A little bit of water in the bottom of the bowl will help keep them fresh. Place the bowl of flowers, along with tools and instructions for crafting the leis, on a small table near the entrance to your party. Guests can create their own leis as they arrive, wear them throughout the party, and then take them home as a memento of their trip to Motunui!

Don't forget your signature drink! Add the punch and the juices to a large drink dispenser and let them chill in the fridge. Create a drink station with glasses and a bowl of lime slices for garnishing. Take the pitcher out of the fridge and add it to the drink station as the first guest arrives.

Enjoy your day on Motunui!

never

second star
to the right
cookies

Peter Pan
"Never Grow Up" Birthday Party

Tinkerbell's pixie punch

captain hook's treasure

mermaid lagoon

lost boys hors d'oeuvres

Peter Pan
"Never Grow Up" Birthday Party

EVENT OVERVIEW

FOR THE MENU

- Lost Boys Hors d'Oeuvres
- The Jolly Roger Cheese Board
- Second Star to the Right Cookies
- Captain Hook's Treasure
- Tinker Bell's Pixie Punch

FOR THE SPACE

- The Jolly Roger Serving Bowl
- "Never Grow Up" Party Backdrop

FOR FUN

- Find the Guest: A Never Land Mix-and-Mingle Game

Welcome to Never Land, home to Peter Pan, Captain Hook, and a rascally collection of pirates, Lost Boys, fairies, and more! In Never Land, no one ever has to grow up. So for this year's birthday, why not indulge your inner Peter Pan? Just follow the second star to the right and head straight on to this Peter Pan–inspired birthday party.

Peter Pan is full of fun elements that can be easily adapted to crafts and decor. Your party will feature a Jolly Roger Serving Bowl and a whimsical backdrop covered with stars. The ambience is casual, with a menu of handheld foods and small bites so guests can mingle and chat while enjoying a signature drink that is as sparkly as it is tasty.

Remember to think happy thoughts—we're off to Never Land!

(**CLOCKWISE FROM TOP LEFT**) Second Star to the Right Cookies; Lost Boys Hors d'Oeuvres; green soda bottles with red feathers make a fun decorative element; Captain Hook's Treasure; Tinker Bell's Pixie Punch; The Jolly Roger Cheese Board

LOST BOYS HORS D'OEUVRES

- **Chicken nuggets or bite-size appetizer of your choice**

Prepare according to package directions. Use toothpicks to serve, and enjoy immediately.

THE JOLLY ROGER CHEESE BOARD

- **Various small fruits, such as blackberries or grapes**
- **Various cheeses, such as cheddar, smoked Gouda, or Colby Jack**
- **Various salami or prosciutto meats, such as peppered salami, sweet soppressata, or dry coppa**
- **Various herbed or flatbread crackers**

SPECIAL SUPPLIES:

- **The Jolly Roger Serving Bowl (page 144)**

Arrange a selection of fruits, cheeses, meats, and crackers in your Jolly Roger serving bowl. Start with the crackers. Arrange them in different groups around the boat, then fill in with fruit. Add the cheese and meats.

Note

Make your own menu labels for this party or download the Peter Pan Menu Cards from our online resources.

SECOND STAR TO THE RIGHT COOKIES

YIELD: 24 COOKIES

- 3 cups all-purpose flour
- 2 teaspoons baking powder
- ½ teaspoon salt
- 2 sticks unsalted butter, cold
- 1 cup sugar
- 1 egg
- 1 teaspoon pure vanilla extract
- ½ teaspoon pure almond extract
- White cookie icing for decorating
- Edible gold paint for decorating

SPECIAL SUPPLIES:

- Star cookie cutter
- Small paintbrush

1. Preheat oven to 350°F. Line a baking sheet with parchment paper and set aside.

2. In a large bowl, combine the flour, baking powder, and salt.

3. In a separate bowl, use hand mixer to cream together the butter and sugar. Once the butter and sugar are combined, add the egg and extracts, and continue to mix.

4. Add the flour mixture gradually (about 1 cup at a time) and beat until a crumbly dough forms.

5. Scoop the dough out of the bowl and knead it together with your hands as you transfer to a floured surface.

6. Roll out the dough and cut out cookies with star cookie cutter. Place on prepared baking sheets and freeze for 10 minutes before baking.

7. Remove from freezer and bake for 10 to 12 minutes, until edges are slightly golden.

8. Allow cookies to cool slightly on baking sheet, and then transfer to a wire rack to finish cooling.

9. Once the cookies have cooled completely, cover faces of cookies with white icing: Pour store-bought icing into a small bowl and dip the front of each cookie into the icing (be careful not to dip too deep— you only want to cover the face of each cookie). Let dry completely.

10. Once cookie icing is dry, paint on splotches of edible gold paint using a small paintbrush. Set aside to dry.

CAPTAIN HOOK'S TREASURE

- **Cream sandwich cookies in two sizes, large and mini**
- **Edible gold luster dust for dusting**

1. Brush gold luster dust on cookies.
2. Arrange on a platter of your choosing to create a hoard of pirate medallions. Captain Hook might be disappointed to find out these are delicious snacks instead of real treasure—but your guests won't be!

TINKER BELL'S PIXIE PUNCH

YIELD: 18 SERVINGS

- **One 64-ounce carton white-cranberry peach juice**
- **Honeydew-melon-flavored syrup for coloring**
- **1 liter club soda**
- **Edible pearl dust for dusting (optional)**

Pour juice into a large pitcher. Add the syrup, stirring continuously until the color is a vibrant green. Chill until ready to serve. Add club soda just before serving. Optional: Use edible pearl dust to make the drink sparkly when you stir it. Be sure to use clear glasses to show off the full effect!

Tip

This recipe can be made with a different juice, but it's important to choose a clear juice so the drink will take on the green color of the honeydew syrup.

THE JOLLY ROGER SERVING BOWL

- **Wooden dowels**
- **Hot glue gun**
- **Ivory cotton fabric (about 1 yard)**
- **Jolly Roger Pirate Ship Flag** ⊙
- **Drill**
- **Drill bit**
- **Short wooden pedestal**
- **Large wooden dough bowl**

1. Create the "mast" of your ship by laying out one long wooden dowel and placing three other dowels across it, spaced according to how much drape you want in your sails. Secure your "crossbars" to your mast with your hot glue gun and let dry.

2. Cut a long piece of fabric the same width as your crossbars. This can be a little ragged around the edges—it's a pirate ship, after all. Hot glue the top edge of the fabric to the top crossbar.

3. Hot glue the fabric to the second crossbar, allowing for some excess fabric to hang between the two bars to create a billowy topsail. Repeat this process for the bottom sail and trim any leftover fabric from the bottom crossbar.

Download the Jolly Roger Pirate Ship Flag. Print out and attach to the top of the mast with tape or glue. ⊙

4. Drill a hole in the top of the wooden pedestal just wide enough for the dowel to fit tightly.

5. Place the mast in the center of your bowl. Fill the boat with your cheese board offerings and enjoy!

DISNEY FUN FACT

Captain Hook was not the original villain of the story. In early drafts of J.M. Barrie's play, Peter Pan himself was the villain. Barrie later expanded Captain Hook's role because of children's fascination with pirates.

"NEVER GROW UP" PARTY BACKDROP

- "Never Grow Up" Backdrop Poster ⬇
- 20-by-30-inch foam core board
- Spray glue
- Scissors
- Glitter card stock
- Clear string
- Tape
- Wooden branch

1. Download and print the "Never Grow Up" Backdrop Poster from our online resources. ⬇
2. Attach to foam core board with spray glue.
3. Cut stars from glitter card stock.
4. Hang stars from wooden branch using tape and clear string, and attach the branch to the top of your backdrop.

Tip

To make your backdrop freestanding, simply attach two PVC poles to the back with duct tape and stick in the ground.

DISNEY FUN FACT

Nana was originally meant to travel to Never Land with the children. She was going to have her own plotline where she chased Tinker Bell.

FIND THE GUEST: A NEVER LAND MIX-AND-MINGLE GAME

- **Find the Guest Game Cards** ⊙
- **White card stock**
- **Scissors**

Download our Find the Guest Game Cards from our online resources, print on white card stock, and cut out. ⊙

6. Let your guests mix and mingle to fill in the questions.

Tip

Offer a special prize of your choosing to the first person to fill out their card completely.

Find a Friend in Never Land

Time to mingle! Talk to your fellow guests to find someone who . . .

——————— Shares your birthday month

——————— Has had a dream in which they were flying

——————— Speaks more than one language

——————— Has visited London

——————— Has owned a Saint Bernard dog

——————— Had a nanny growing up

——————— Shares your first initial

——————— Is wearing green

——————— Shares your favorite TV show

——————— Played the same sport growing up

——————— Has been on a pirate ship

——————— Has seen a real crocodile

——————— Has gone camping

——————— Has made plans to run away from home

——————— Has on the same color shoes as you

——————— Has dressed up as a fairy

——————— Wishes they had magical fairy dust

——————— Has had a secret clubhouse

When you find a match, have them sign your card. The first to fill out their card completely gets a special prize!

Putting It All Together

TWO OR MORE WEEKS BEFORE:

Send out invitations to your friends. They will not want to miss this adventure!

Purchase all your craft supplies. It's best to start shopping for these items early in case some of them, like the wooden dough bowl, need time to ship.

ONE WEEK BEFORE:

Gather your decor and start to plan your table. A burlap tablecloth is a great base for this theme because it feels a little rough-and-tumble. The Lost Boys would love it! If you don't have a burlap tablecloth, a simple piece of burlap is a fine alternative. As far as tableware goes, it's best to stick with simple items, as there is already a lot of color in this party. Natural wood finishes and simple white serving dishes should hit the mark. Since this is a casual party, paper plates and napkins are fine. Get star-shaped plates and star-print napkins for an extra dose of fun. And because this menu is full of finger foods, no cutlery is needed.

Create the crafts. Make your backdrop, attach the stars to the branch, and attach the branch to your backdrop. Create the Jolly Roger Serving Bowl. This is a surprisingly easy craft, but it looks really impressive when it's complete.

TWO DAYS BEFORE:

Purchase all the food and drinks you need for your menu. Be sure to chill all your drink ingredients so they will be nice and cold on the day of the party.

Now is the time to finalize any little extra elements you're bringing to your party. One fun accent that is quite easy to create is a set of little pixie hollows. These are simple potted succulents sprinkled with fairy dust (*ahem*, gold glitter). Gather the supplies for these now, but wait to add the glitter until an hour before the party so they stay twinkly all night.

Another fun idea is to tie red feathers to green soda bottles as a clever callout to Peter Pan's hat. And a bowl of plastic party compasses makes for a fun favor so your guests can find their way back home after their trip to Never Land.

In terms of flowers, nothing on this table should look too arranged. Instead of bouquets, go with balls of succulent greenery and other small potted ferns and shrubs. For a centerpiece, try a natural arrangement of aloe, small ferns, and clippings from the shrubbery in your yard. We arranged ours in a faux-crocodile-skin vase and paired it with a spray-painted crocodile and a small clock to create a fun centerpiece inspired by Tick Tock the Crocodile.

If using our Peter Pan Menu Cards, download the files from our online resources, and print and cut them out so they are ready to use.

ONE DAY BEFORE:

Preparing some of your menu the day before will leave you more time to set up and decorate on the day of your party. Bake and decorate the Second Star to the Right Cookies. Allowing them to dry overnight will ensure they will be beautiful when they are stacked and displayed. Create Captain Hook's Treasure by brushing the gold luster dust on the cream sandwich cookies. You can also cut up the meat and cheeses for the cheese board. Store these overnight in separate containers in the refrigerator.

THE DAY OF:

Set your table and arrange your serving pieces. Place your pixie hollow arrangements and your Tick Tock Croc centerpiece on the table. Place a stack of paper plates in the shape of stars on the table. Add paper napkins with foil stars on them and a cup of toothpicks for the Lost Boys Hors d'Oeuvres.

This menu is light on cooking, so you will have plenty of time to play with your table arrangement. There is no wrong way to display the food. Have fun with it! Set out your Second Star to the Right Cookies and Captain Hook's Treasure. Arrange your cheese board offerings in your Jolly Roger Serving Bowl and set it out in a prominent spot on the table. Set out your menu cards. Fifteen minutes before your party starts, rewarm your Lost Boys Hors d'Oeuvres in the oven for about ten minutes.

Don't forget your signature drink! Add juice and syrup to a pitcher and chill in your refrigerator. Right before the party, add the club soda and pearl dust. For extra fun, serve these drinks in glasses rimmed with green sugar sprinkles.

Enjoy your Never Land adventure!

Disney Vile Villains
Halloween Pumpkin-Carving Party

Disney Vile Villains
Halloween Pumpkin-Carving Party

EVENT OVERVIEW

FOR THE MENU

- Maleficent's Spicy Dragon-Fire Tomato Soup
- Scar's Boneyard Breadsticks
- Evil Queen's Poison Apples
- Evil Queen's "Sleeping Death" Pistachio Pudding
- Ursula's Sea Witch Brew
- Disney's Vile Villain Cupcakes

FOR THE SPACE

- Sea Witch Punch Bowl
- Maleficent Welcome Wreath
- Pick Your Poison Backdrop

FOR FUN

- Pumpkin-Carving Tool Kits
- Vile Villains Playlist

Without a villain, there is no story—and Disney has some of the best villains around. From *Sleeping Beauty*'s malicious fairy Maleficent to *The Little Mermaid*'s cruel sea witch Ursula to the ambitious Scar from *The Lion King*, this is the best group of baddies you'll find. This Halloween, let the Disney villains inspire your worst nightmares as your friends gather for a night of spooky fun, complete with frightening food, diabolical decor, and pumpkin carving!

For those who enjoy the darker side of life, we've got all the ingredients for one wicked party. Poison apples? Check. Smoking beverage? Check. Playlist of jaunty villain tunes expounding their evil deeds? Check! Have your guests bring their own pumpkins, while you provide the carving supplies and the ambience with showstopping crafts like the Maleficent Welcome Wreath and the Sea Witch Punch Bowl.

Summon your squad, pick your pumpkin, and get ready to celebrate Halloween with Disney's most vile villains!

(CLOCKWISE FROM TOP LEFT) Set up your pumpkin-carving station away from your food table; Maleficent Welcome Wreath; Disney's Vile Villain Cupcakes; Evil Queen's "Sleeping Death" Pistachio Pudding; Pumpkin-Carving Tool Kits; Sea Witch Punch Bowl

DON'T BE AFRAID

I'M SURROUNDED BY IDIOTS

IT'S GOOD TO BE

YOU POOR UNFORTUNATE

I'M SURROUNDED BY IDIOTS

DRAGON FIRE
TOMATO SOUP

Tip

Want more heat? Or less? Adjust the amount of cayenne pepper to taste. Ideally, though, this should have a little kick—it is dragon-fire soup, after all!

MALEFICENT'S SPICY DRAGON-FIRE TOMATO SOUP

YIELD: 12 SERVINGS

- 2 tablespoons extra-virgin olive oil
- 2 tablespoons unsalted butter
- 1 yellow onion, chopped
- 3 cloves garlic, minced
- 5 large tomatoes, coarsely chopped
- 1½ teaspoons sugar
- 1 tablespoon tomato paste
- 1 teaspoon cayenne pepper (or adjust to your heat preference)
- ¼ cup chopped fresh basil leaves, plus more for garnishing
- 3 cups chicken stock
- 1 tablespoon salt
- 2 teaspoons freshly ground black pepper
- ¾ cup heavy cream
- Croutons for garnishing

1. Combine the olive oil and butter in a large stockpot over medium-low heat.
2. Once the oil and butter have heated, add the onion and garlic and cook until the onion is translucent and the garlic fragrant, about 2 to 3 minutes.
3. Add the tomatoes, sugar, tomato paste, cayenne pepper, basil, chicken stock, salt, and pepper to the pot and turn the heat up to medium-high. Stir frequently as the soup comes to a boil.
4. Lower the heat, and simmer, uncovered, for 30 to 40 minutes.
5. Working in batches, pour the soup into a blender. Do not overfill the blender, so hot liquid does not escape the opening in the blender cover and burn you. Alternatively, use an immersion blender to blend the soup in the pot until completely smooth.
6. Add the cream to the blended soup, and let simmer an additional 5 minutes.
7. Serve in individual goblets and top with basil, croutons, or both.

SCAR'S BONEYARD BREADSTICKS

YIELD: 12 SERVINGS

- 12 to 15 soft Italian breadsticks
- 8 ounces prosciutto
- Olive oil for drizzling
- Fresh cracked pepper, to taste

1. Preheat oven to 350°F.
2. Wrap one slice of prosciutto around one breadstick. Place wrapped breadstick on sheet pan lined with parchment paper. Repeat until you have used all of the prosciutto.
3. Drizzle olive oil over wrapped breadsticks and top with fresh cracked pepper.
4. Bake for 8 minutes or until prosciutto is warm. Serve immediately.

EVIL QUEEN'S POISON APPLES

YIELD: 6 SERVINGS

- 8 small red apples
- 2 cups granulated sugar
- ½ cup light corn syrup
- ¾ cup water
- Red food coloring, to preferred color

SPECIAL SUPPLIES:

- 8 wooden branches, washed and dried

1. Insert a wooden branch through the top and into the center of each apple. The apples should stay on when you pick them up by the stick.

2. Heat sugar, corn syrup, water, and food coloring in a saucepan over medium-high heat. Use a candy thermometer to bring the mixture to a boil and to a temperature of 302°F (hard crack candy temperature), which will take around 20 minutes. There is no need to stir while the mixture is boiling.

3. Once the syrup reaches 302°F, remove from heat, and quickly dip each apple into the hot liquid, turning thoroughly to coat the entire fruit. Pull apple out of syrup. Let cool for 30 seconds and dip a second time to ensure a smooth candy shell.

4. After the second dip, briefly hold the apple upside down to reverse the pooling of the coating, then transfer to a parchment-lined baking sheet to cool.

5. Let stand until the candy has cooled completely and hardened, about 30 minutes, before serving.

Tip

You might be tempted to make these ahead of time, but the longer they sit, the more the candy will soften. So make these the day of the event!

DISNEY FUN FACT

The Evil Queen from *Snow White and the Seven Dwarfs* was the first character to speak in a full-length animated feature.

EVIL QUEEN'S "SLEEPING DEATH" PISTACHIO PUDDING

YIELD: 12 SERVINGS

- Two 3.4-ounce packages instant pistachio pudding mix
- One 20-ounce can crushed pineapple
- One 16-ounce carton lite frozen whipped topping, thawed
- One 10-ounce bag mini marshmallows
- Green food coloring to desired color
- Green sugar pearl candy sprinkles for garnishing
- Cherries, stems trimmed short, for garnishing

SPECIAL SUPPLIES:

- Small plastic cauldrons

1. Combine pistachio pudding mix and pineapple in a large bowl.
2. Fold in thawed whipped topping and marshmallows.
3. Add food coloring several drops at a time, stirring, until the pudding reaches your desired color.
4. Fill small plastic cauldrons with pudding and refrigerate to chill.
5. Just before serving, add green sugar pearl candy sprinkles to look like bubbles, and top each cauldron with a fresh red cherry to look like a small apple bobbing in the potion.

Tip

Do not handle dry ice with bare hands. Use tongs only. A small piece is plenty for one drink.

URSULA'S SEA WITCH BREW

YIELD: 12 SERVINGS

- 2 liters club soda
- One 12-ounce can frozen limeade concentrate
- One 64-ounce bottle grape juice
- One 64-ounce bottle cranberry juice
- Dry ice for effect (optional)

1. Combine club soda, frozen limeade, grape juice, and cranberry juice in your Sea Witch Punch Bowl (page 161). Add a small piece of dry ice to the bowl just before the party starts to create a spooky effect.
2. To serve, use tongs to add a small piece of dry ice to each drink, and wait until it fully dissolves before drinking.

DISNEY'S VILE VILLAIN CUPCAKES

YIELD: 12 SERVINGS

CUPCAKES:

- One 15.25-ounce box of red velvet cake mix
- 4 eggs
- 1 cup buttermilk
- ⅓ cup vegetable oil, or the amount called for on the box

TOPPERS:

- Two 16-ounce cans white icing
- Red fondant
- Yellow fondant
- Edible gold luster dust for dusting
- One 16-ounce can chocolate icing
- Black food coloring
- Black fondant
- White candy melts
- Purple food coloring

SPECIAL SUPPLIES:

- Gold card stock
- Tape
- Skull candy mold

TO MAKE THE CUPCAKES:

1. Preheat oven to 350°F. Prepare a cupcake pan by greasing the inside of each cup or adding cupcake liners.
2. Combine cake mix, eggs, buttermilk, and vegetable oil in bowl and mix until well combined. Add batter to cupcake pan, filling each cup ⅔ full.
3. Bake for 15 to 18 minutes or until toothpick comes out clean. Remove from oven and let cool completely.

TO MAKE THE QUEEN OF HEARTS TOPPER:

1. Pipe white icing on top of your cupcakes.
2. Shape small balls of red fondant into hearts and set one on each cupcake atop the icing.
3. Create small crowns from yellow fondant and dust each with edible gold luster dust. Attach one crown to each heart using icing as a "glue."

TO MAKE THE CRUELLA DE VIL TOPPER:

Pipe white icing spikes on one half of each cupcake and black icing spikes on the other half to look like Cruella's hair.

TO MAKE THE CAPTAIN HOOK TOPPER:

1. Color chocolate icing with black food coloring to make black icing. Pipe black icing on top of your cupcakes.

2. Top the black icing with a layer of white icing using a petal piping tip to create the ruffles of Captain Hook's shirt.

3. Make a small ball out of black fondant; this will form the base of the hook that sits atop each cupcake.

4. To make the hook, cut a toothpick to 1½ inches, and wrap a small ball of black fondant around one end, leaving about ½ inch of the toothpick visible. Roll out the ball into a long skinny worm, letting the end come to a point. Shape the end into a hook and let dry.

5. Dust with edible gold glitter and then attach the hook to the base by sticking the toothpick into the base. Set your hooks on top of the white icing on each cupcake and sprinkle with a small amount of gold luster dust for added effect.

TO MAKE THE DR. FACILIER TOPPER:

1. Melt white candy melts according to package directions. Pour melted candy into skull mold and let harden in refrigerator for 15 minutes.

2. In the meantime, color white icing purple using purple food coloring. Pipe the icing onto your cupcakes.

3. Add a candy skull to the top of your icing on each cupcake.

For the Space

SEA WITCH PUNCH BOWL

- **14-inch-diameter black plastic cauldron**
- **Painter's tape**
- **Purple spray paint**
- **Gold spray paint**
- **Seashell**
- **1 yard black fabric**
- **1 yard purple fabric**
- **Sewing tools: pins, thread, and sewing machine**
- **Ursula's Tentacles Sewing Templates** ⊕
- **Poly-fill stuffing**
- **Hot glue gun**
- **Silver sequin confetti, large**
- **Cake stand**
- **Black baker's twine**
- **White craft feathers**
- **White craft feathers with glitter tips**
- **Black duct tape**

1. Remove handle from cauldron. Use painter's tape to create the bustline of Ursula's dress, then fully cover the rest of the bottom of the cauldron with tape to protect it from paint.

2. Spray-paint the top of the cauldron purple and let dry.

3. Spray-paint the seashell gold and let dry.

4. To create the tentacles, place the black fabric on top of the purple fabric with right sides of fabric facing each other. Pin together with straight pins if helpful to hold the fabric together.

5. Cut out the Large Ursula's Tentacles Sewing Template. Lay fabric down on flat surface with black fabric on top and purple fabric on bottom. Trace four tentacles on the pinned-together fabrics, keeping your outlines close together so you don't waste fabric. Cut them out, and set aside. ⊕

6. Cut out the Small Ursula's Tentacles Sewing Template. For this set of tentacles, make sure purple fabric is on top and black fabric is on bottom (so that your tentacles curve in opposite directions). Trace three tentacles on the pinned-together fabrics, cut out them out, and set aside. ⊕

In sewing, the *right side* of fabric refers to the side that will be on the outside of the finished product.

7. Working with one tentacle at a time, attach the two pieces of fabric by sewing along the edges of the tentacles (with right sides of fabric still facing each other). Leave only the top open for now; this is how you will add the stuffing. Flip sewn tentacles inside out so the outer sides are now showing.

8. Stuff each tentacle with poly-fill stuffing. Make sure you get the stuffing down into the tip of each tentacle. Once the tentacles are stuffed, hot glue the top openings closed.

9. Hot glue large silver sequin confetti to the purple side of each tentacle to create the effect of suction cups on the undersides of the tentacles.

10. Place cauldron on top of cake stand for height. Hot glue each tentacle to the bottom of the cauldron near the edge. Start with large tentacles, evenly spacing them around the entire cauldron. Fill in the spaces with the small tentacles and hot glue them in place.

11. Tie a length of black baker's twine to the cauldron using the holes from the handle you removed. The length you need will depend on the width of your cauldron; it should be long enough so the shell hangs like Ursula's necklace.

12. Hot glue the shell to the cauldron in the middle of the length of twine.

13. To make Ursula's hair, lay the white craft feathers down in a flat, overlapping pile. Cover the ends with black duct tape to secure them together. Then lay the glitter-tip feathers on top of the white feathers, and secure in place with duct tape. Now duct tape the entire strip into the top inside of the cauldron to look like Ursula's hair.

14. Hand-wash the inside of the cauldron before serving your punch and enjoy!

MALEFICENT WELCOME WREATH

- **Maleficent Horns Template** ⬇
- **14-inch green extruded foam wreath, smooth with rounded edges**
- **Black duct tape**
- **Newspaper**
- **½ yard black fabric**
- **Black feather wreath with foam base**
- **Straight pins**
- **Decorative black crow**
- **Hot glue**
- **Maleficent Welcome Sign** ⬇
- **White card stock**

1. Print out the Maleficent Horns Template. This will be your guide as you shape and create the horns. ⬇

2. Break the foam wreath in half. Lay one half of the foam wreath down on the template. This will be the structure for the bottom of the horn. Locate the area on the template where the shape of the horn starts to curve back in toward the center, and break the foam wreath again at that place. Duct tape the two foam pieces together to form the basic structure of the horn. Repeat for the other horn.

3. Wrap newspaper around the taped foam wreath pieces, and shape the rest of the horn up to the tip. Use the template as your guide to get the right shape, and build up the thickness at the bottom with extra layers of newspaper. Duct tape to secure shape. Repeat for both horns.

4. Cut black fabric in roughly 6-inch strips. Working with one horn at a time, wrap the fabric strips around the horn, starting at the base and securing each piece with black duct tape. Overlap each strip as you work your way up the horn until the entire shape is wrapped. Secure the end of the fabric to the top of the horn using hot glue or black duct tape.

5. Attach the horns to the top of a feather wreath using straight pins and black duct tape.

6. Use a pin or hot glue to attach the crow to the foam base of the feather wreath.

7. Print out the Maleficent Welcome Sign on white card stock, and secure it to your wreath with hot glue. ⬇

8. Hang your wreath on your front door to welcome your guests to the party with a special message from the Mistress of All Evil!

DISNEY FUN FACT

Maleficent means "evildoing" in Latin.

PICK YOUR POISON BACKDROP

- **Pick Your Poison Backdrop Poster** ⊙
- **Black poster board (optional)**
- **Scissors**
- **32-by-40-inch black foam core board**
- **Spray glue**
- **Knife or razor blade**

1. Download the Pick Your Poison Backdrop Poster from our online resources. ⊙

2. Print the backdrop poster at your local photo printer on poster paper. This is a large-format poster, so it will likely need to be shipped to you.

3. If desired, glue the printed poster onto a sheet of black poster board to reinforce it. Then cut out the image, removing the excess paper at the top of the poster to create the custom shape.

4. Place the poster facedown on the ground, and use spray glue to glue the foam core board to the bottom half of the poster, allowing the top to extend beyond the top edge of the board. Use a knife or razor blade to cut away the extra board.

5. Place your poster behind your table and admire the chilling effect!

Tip

Drywall saws are the best tool for cutting the top off a pumpkin.

PUMPKIN-CARVING TOOL KITS

Make one for each guest.

- Paper favor boxes
- Disney Villain Box Labels ⬇
- White card stock
- Foam square stickers
- Black paper shreds
- Pumpkin-carving scoops
- Pumpkin-carving detail knives
- Candles

1. Download our Disney Villain Box Labels from our online resources, and print them out on card stock. These are 2½ by 3 inches and should fit nicely on small favor boxes. ⬇

2. Cut out each label, and use foam square stickers to attach one to each favor box.

3. Fill each box with black paper shreds, and add one carving scoop, one carving detail knife, and a candle.

4. Let each guest choose a tool kit with their favorite villain on it!

VILE VILLAINS PLAYLIST

Set the mood for your party with a playlist of your favorite Disney villain songs!

PLAYLIST

1. "Poor Unfortunate Souls," *The Little Mermaid*
2. "Friends on the Other Side," *The Princess and The Frog*
3. "Oogie Boogie's Song," *The Nightmare Before Christmas*
4. "Cruella De Vil," *101 Dalmations*
5. "Gaston," *Beauty and the Beast*
6. "Be Prepared," *The Lion King*
7. "Mother Knows Best," *Tangled*
8. "Savages," *Pocahontas*
9. "Prince Ali (Reprise)," *Aladdin*
10. "Hellfire," *The Hunchback of Notre Dame*
11. "The Elegant Captain Hook," *Peter Pan*
12. "Trust in Me," *The Jungle Book*
13. "Shiny," *Moana*
14. "Painting the Roses Red" and "Who's Been Painting My Roses Red?" *Alice in Wonderland*

DISNEY FUN FACT

Nearly all Disney villains wear black, purple, red, or some variation of the three. They also frequently have lime-green eyes or use magic that appears lime green.

TWO OR MORE WEEKS BEFORE:

Send out invitations to your friends to get this party on their calendar! Make it a BYOP party . . . Bring Your Own Pumpkin. Since people will want some time to enjoy their creations postcarving, we recommend hosting this party the week before Halloween. This will also help free up any scheduling issue for parents with trick-or-treating kids.

Purchase all your craft supplies, and create your playlist for the party. Craft the Maleficent Welcome Wreath and Sea Witch Punch Bowl. These are not difficult crafts, but they will take some time. Start early so you don't feel rushed as your party date creeps closer.

Order a poster of the Pick Your Poison Backdrop. When it arrives, craft the backdrop so it's ready to use. You can also download and print out the menu cards.

ONE WEEK BEFORE:

Gather your decor and serving pieces. When selecting your serving pieces, stick to classic Disney villain colors like black, purple, lime green, and red. These colors pop nicely against a purple crushed velvet tablecloth. Black goblets are a fun, easy way to serve individual servings of tomato soup. Try to find the most ornate set you can—Maleficent does enjoy her drama, after all. Another easy dramatic touch is to add jewel scatter in black, green, and purple to your cupcake platter. A skeleton hand is perfect for displaying one of the Evil Queen's Poison Apples, while mini black cauldrons are a fun way to serve the Evil Queen's "Sleeping Death" Pistachio Pudding.

TWO DAYS BEFORE:

Purchase all the food you need for your menu (except dry ice), and while you're at it, pick out a nice pumpkin for yourself. Be sure to chill all your drink ingredients so they will be nice and cold on your party day. Purchase or collect the wooden branches for your poison apples, wash them, and let dry.

ONE DAY BEFORE:

Preparing some of your menu the day before will leave you more time to set up and decorate on the day of your party. Prepare Maleficent's Spicy Dragon-Fire Tomato Soup, and refrigerate overnight. You can heat it up on the stove the following day. You can also make the pistachio pudding and fill the cauldrons. These will keep fresh in the refrigerator overnight.

Bake the Disney's Vile Villain cupcakes today, but wait to decorate them until the day of your

party. Store your undecorated baked cupcakes in an airtight container. You can also make the edible cupcake toppers, and divide and color the icings you will be using. Then everything will be ready to decorate your cupcakes the morning of your party.

Create your Pumpkin-Carving Tool Kits so they're ready to go for the following day. It's also not a bad idea to have a couple of extra large knives and scoops handy for the initial carving and cleaning out of the pumpkins.

THE DAY OF:

Start the day by decorating your cupcakes. Once they are iced and decorated, they will be fine sitting out on your platter until your party tonight. Make your candy apples next. Do not store these in the refrigerator. They are best stored in a cool dry place until party time.

Carving pumpkins is an activity best done outside, so we recommend setting up this party in your backyard. Cover a sturdy table in butcher paper, place a garbage bag in a bucket, and place the bucket in the center of the table for the pumpkin guts. When the party's over, dump the bag in the garbage (or the guts in your com-post!), and roll up and toss the butcher paper. Who doesn't love an easy cleanup?

Set up a separate table for your food and drink. Cover with your purple crushed velvet tablecloth and add your backdrop and menu cards. Put out your pumpkin-carving kits, your punch bowl, and your pumpkin. Hang your wreath on your front door to welcome your guests to the party!

Time to purchase the dry ice. Dry ice does not keep overnight, so wait until a few hours before the party to purchase it so you will have enough

for the whole night. Store the dry ice in a dry cooler, never in your freezer. Dry ice will burn you if you touch it with your bare hands, so remember to use tongs. It might seem like a bit of a hassle, but your friends will love the spooky effect!

Reheat the tomato soup on the stove over medium heat. Prepare Scar's Boneyard Breadsticks, but wait to drizzle the oil and bake until fifteen minutes before your party starts.

Don't forget your signature drink! Add your punch and the juices to your punch bowl. Keep a cooler of dry ice and tongs nearby to add a small piece to each glass of punch as you serve it (remember to let it dis-solve fully before drinking).

MENU

ANNA'S HAM, EGG, AND
CHEESE CROISSANT SANDWICHES
STRAWBERRY FROZEN HEARTS
ARENDELLE WINTER WAFFLE BAR
OLAF'S SNOWBALLS
ELSA'S EGGNOGG

Chocolate
"FOR STUFFING YOUR FACE"

anna

MENU

ANNA'S HAM, EGG, AN

Frozen
Winter Wonderland Holiday Brunch

Menu

Anna's Ham, Egg, and
Cheese Croissant Sandwiches

Strawberry Frozen Hearts

Arendelle Winter Waffle Bar

Olaf's Snowballs

Elsa's Eggnogg

Chocolate "for stuffing your face"

Frozen
Winter Wonderland Holiday Brunch

EVENT OVERVIEW

FOR THE MENU

- Strawberry Frozen Hearts
- Anna's Ham, Egg, and Cheese Croissant Sandwiches
- Arendelle Winter Waffle Bar
- Olaf's Snowballs
- Elsa's Eggnog

FOR THE SPACE

- Iced Menu Cards
- Snowball Place Cards

FOR FUN

- Vanilla Hot Chocolate Station
- Face-Stuffing Chocolate Favors

In *Frozen*, Queen Elsa's powerful magic turns the sunny summertime landscape of Arendelle into an icy winter wonderland. While this isn't much fun for the citizens of Arendelle, it does make for a great party theme, especially for a host looking to bring a unique twist to a holiday gathering.

The holidays are an undeniably busy time of year, but it's important to take some time to spend with your friends and loved ones. This *Frozen* Winter Wonderland Holiday Brunch is perfect for a small group of close friends looking to unwind from the busyness of the season and "let it go." The menu is a treat—it includes a winter waffle bar, eggnog that looks like melting snow, and delicious ham-and-cheese croissant sandwiches (for Anna). The decor is suitably icy, but the Vanilla Hot Chocolate Station should help you keep warm. And if you're feeling extra festive, the toppings are perfect for building a snowman!

(**CLOCKWISE FROM TOP LEFT**) Strawberry Frozen Hearts; Elsa's Eggnog; make a melting snowman for your vanilla hot chocolate; pile on the toppings with our Arendelle Winter Waffle Bar; Face-Stuffing Chocolate Favors; Snowball Place Cards

natalie

Menu

Chocolate
"FOR STUFFING YOUR FACE"

DISNEY
FUN FACT

The design of Arendelle is heavily influenced by the country of Norway. A Norwegian pattern called rosemaling can be seen throughout the movie.

STRAWBERRY FROZEN HEARTS

- **Fresh strawberries**
- **White chocolate candy melts**
- **White candy sprinkles**

1. Wash and dry the strawberries.
2. Remove stems and cut strawberries in half to make a heart shape.
3. Melt chocolate candy according to package directions. Line a baking sheet with parchment paper, and arrange strawberry halves on it, cut sides down. Drizzle melted chocolate onto strawberries and sprinkle with candy sprinkles while still wet. Let dry completely before serving.

ANNA'S HAM, EGG, AND CHEESE CROISSANT SANDWICHES

YIELD: 8 SANDWICHES

- **8 eggs**
- **4 tablespoons Dijon mustard**
- **2 tablespoons honey**
- **2 tablespoons brown sugar**
- **8 croissants, split**
- **16 slices provolone cheese**
- **2 pounds shaved deli ham**

1. Preheat oven to 350°F.
2. Cook scrambled eggs to your preferred consistency and set aside on a plate.
3. In a small bowl, combine mustard, honey, and brown sugar to create a simple honey-mustard spread. Spread the mixture on cut side of the bottom half of each croissant.
4. Layer a slice of cheese, two slices of ham, one portion of scrambled egg, and another slice of cheese inside each croissant. Sandwich the croissants back together and arrange on a rimmed baking sheet.
5. Cover the sheet in foil and bake for 10 to 15 minutes. Serve immediately.

ARENDELLE
WINTER WAFFLE BAR

YIELD: 8 SERVINGS

- **Frozen waffles**
- **Various flavored syrups for topping**
- **Savory bites such as bacon and sausage for topping**
- **Fresh fruit such as blackberries, blueberries, and strawberries for topping**
- **Sweets such as cinnamon rolls and granola for topping**

1. Cook waffles according to package directions.
2. Cook bacon and sausage.
3. Cut bacon, sausage, fruit, and cinnamon rolls into bite-size pieces for serving.
4. Serve all toppings in individual bowls, alongside cooked waffles. Let guests design their own waffle creations.

DISNEY
FUN FACT

Elsa's iconic power ballad "Let It Go" was written in one day. The song has since been recorded in forty-one languages.

OLAF'S SNOWBALLS

- **Frozen cream puffs**
- **Powdered sugar for topping**

Thaw cream puffs and roll in powdered sugar. Serve immediately.

ELSA'S EGGNOG

YIELD: 12 SERVINGS

- **½-gallon carton eggnog**
- **2 liters lemon lime soda, chilled**
- **10 to 12 scoops of vanilla ice cream**
- **Ground nutmeg for garnishing**

1. Combine eggnog and soda in a large drink dispenser.
2. Add scoops of vanilla ice cream to look like melting snow, and garnish with a dash of ground nutmeg.
3. Serve in small glasses.

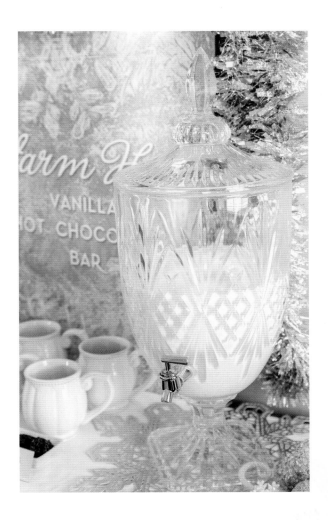

Tip

This signature drink looks amazing served in cut crystal glasses.

ICED MENU CARDS

Make one for each place setting at your table.

- **5-by-7-inch acrylic sheets**
- **White vinyl or white paint pen**
- **Cutting machine, if using vinyl**
- **Transfer tape for vinyl**
- **White shimmery paper**
- **Menu Header Template** ⊕
- **Menu Text Template** ⊕

1. Download the Frozen Menu Header Template and Frozen Menu Text Template from our online resources. ⊕
2. If you own a cutting machine, cut the header from white vinyl and use transfer tape to attach to the top of each acrylic sheet.
3. Print the text for the menu out on shimmery white paper. This special paper can be found at your local craft store.
4. Place the printed menu underneath one acrylic sheet and put one at each place setting.

SNOWBALL PLACE CARDS

Make one for each guest.

- **Glittery round plastic ornaments**
- **Snowball Place Card Name Tags** ⊕
- **Shimmery white paper**
- **Craft knife**

1. Download the Snowball Place Card Name Tags and edit the file to add your guests' names. ⊕
2. Print each name tag on shimmery white paper from your local craft store and cut out.
3. Place the snowball ornament upside down on the table using the ornament topper as a stand so it stays in place. Once you have the snowball placed where it will not roll, use the craft knife to cut a slit in the top of the snowball. Slide the name tag into the slit.
4. Place one at each setting, and let the party begin! These can double as favors as well and can be easily turned into an ornament for a tree or other winter-inspired decor.

Tip

If you don't have a cutting machine, use our template as inspiration, and write the word using a white paint pen.

anna

Chocolate
FOR STUFFING YOUR FACE

Menu

Anna's Ham, Egg, and
Cheese Croissant Sandwiches
Strawberry Frozen Hearts
Arendelle Winter Waffle Bar
Olaf's Snowballs
Elsa's Eggnogg

Warm Hugs

VANILLA
HOT CHOCOLATE
BAR

DO YOU WANT
TO BUILD A
Snowman?

SNOW

EYES

NOSE

ARMS

VANILLA HOT CHOCOLATE STATION

- White hot chocolate
- Variety of toppings to "build a snowman," including mini chocolate chips for eyes, chocolate sprinkles for arms, orange sprinkles for nose, and mini marshmallows for body
- Whipped cream topping
- "Warm Hugs" Vanilla Hot Chocolate Bar Backdrop Poster ⬇
- 20-by-30-inch white foam core board
- Spray glue
- Mugs
- Hot Chocolate Bar Topping Signs ⬇

1. Download the "Warm Hugs" Vanilla Hot Chocolate Bar Backdrop Poster and Hot Chocolate Bar Topping Signs from our online resources. ⬇
2. Print the backdrop poster at your local photo printer on poster paper.
3. Attach poster to foam core board using spray glue.
4. Arrange hot chocolate bar with mugs, toppings, and white hot chocolate.
5. Print out the topping signs on white card stock and place in front of bowls of toppings.

FACE-STUFFING CHOCOLATE FAVORS

- Clear plastic treat boxes
- Chocolates
- Face-Stuffing Chocolate Favor Tags ⬇
- White shimmery paper
- Hole punch
- Ribbon

1. Fill clear plastic treat boxes with chocolates.
2. Download the Face-Stuffing Chocolate Favor Tags from our online resources. ⬇
3. Print these on shimmery white paper from your local craft store and cut out.
4. Punch a hole in each tag and tie to the box of chocolates with ribbon. Place one favor box at each setting for a fun favor and a sweet way to end your event.

DISNEY FUN FACT

In an early version of the film, Anna and Elsa weren't sisters. Anna was a peasant who journeyed to ask Ice Queen Elsa to freeze her broken heart.

Putting It All Together

TWO OR MORE WEEKS BEFORE:

The holidays are a wonderful time to press pause and reconnect with your closest friends. Unfortunately, they're also just about the busiest time of year, so be sure to send out invitations now before everyone's calendars fill up.

Purchase all the craft supplies you will need for this party. If you can't find the acrylic sheets or clear treat boxes at your local craft store, you can order them online, but be sure to allow extra time for shipping.

ONE WEEK BEFORE:

Gather your decor, place settings, and serving pieces. We recommend an ice-blue tablecloth or fabric for your table, against which a mix of white plates, silver cutlery, and crystal glassware will pop nicely. Crystal glasses are a must for this party—the patterns are reminiscent of snowflakes, icicles, and Elsa's magical powers. Snowflake placemats are another fun way to bring your *Frozen* theme to life. Fortunately, all these items are readily available in stores this time of year—and don't have to be too expensive!

Create your acrylic Iced Menu Cards and the Snowball Place Cards. You can also create your Face-Stuffing Chocolate Favors and print out and prep your poster backdrop for your hot chocolate bar.

TWO DAYS BEFORE:

Purchase all the food and drink ingredients you need for your party. Be sure to chill all your drink ingredients so they will be nice and cold on the day of your party.

ONE DAY BEFORE:

Preparing some of your menu the day before will leave you more time to set up and decorate the day of your party. Go ahead and slice the strawberries for the Strawberry Frozen Hearts today, and let them dry on a paper towel. When they are dry, finish the recipe and store in an airtight container overnight in the refrigerator. You also can prep all of the toppings for your waffle bar.

Another thing you can get a jump on is setting up your Vanilla Hot Chocolate Station. While you should definitely wait to put out any food items until the morning of the party, you can set up the space now. Don't forget your poster backdrop!

THE DAY OF:

Start your day by laying your table, beginning with your ice-blue tablecloth and a silver snowflake placemat at each setting. Then layer a white dinner plate, white salad plate, and blue napkin on top of each placemat, and top it off with an acrylic Iced Menu Card and Snowball Place Card. Don't forget your Face-Stuffing Chocolate Favors. Place one at each setting for your friends to take home.

Time to finish preparing your menu. Assemble Anna's Ham, Egg, and Cheese Croissant Sandwiches, but wait to bake them until a half hour before your party begins so they will be nice and warm. Arrange the Strawberry Frozen Hearts on a dish, and add them to the table. Bake the waffles and the savory toppings for the Arendelle Winter Waffle Bar. Arrange all the toppings and waffles for the waffle bar on a large platter and place in the center of your table. While the sandwiches are baking, roll the thawed cream puffs for Olaf's Snowballs in powdered sugar and arrange them in a bowl. Finally, add the hot chocolate and toppings to your hot chocolate station.

Don't forget your signature drink! Pour the ingredients into a crystal drink dispenser, and add the ice cream. Keep a small container of ground nutmeg available for garnishing as the drink is served.

Enjoy your *Frozen* Winter Wonderland Holiday Brunch!

Acknowledgments

To Cole, you are my greatest joy and because of you, there are so many reasons to celebrate! Mom and Dad, your unconditional love and support for all my adventures have given me the courage to follow my dreams, which have brought many unexpected blessings along the way. I love you both. To my friends and family who have encouraged me and shared in the excitement of this book, I am so blessed to have each of you to share the journey with. Thank you for showing up, allowing me to bounce ideas off you, dressing up for a few photos, working tirelessly behind the scenes (Mom!), and being genuinely excited to see it all come together.

To Tori Brinson and Carie Tindill, your gifts and contributions to this book are amazing. Thank you for sharing your time and your talent on this project and for your friendship. You each are a special part of my life and I feel very blessed to call you friends.

I would like to thank the following contributors and cherished friends for providing their talents, time, products, and contributions for the parties featured in this book:

Tori Brinson of Tori Brinson Design for her wonderful floral work, Carie Tindill of Cakeitecture Bakery for her amazing custom cookies and cakes, and Becky Lazenby for her custom sewing.

I'd also like to thank to Swoozie's, Pre Events, Prophouse, and Event Rentals Unlimited for their decor and equipment contributions. A very special thank you to the entire team at Lucy's of Auburn for letting us shoot our Mickey Mouse birthday party on their premises.

In addition, special thanks to models Tori Brinson, Kennedy Brinson, Katie Crow, Aubrey-Joy O'Brien, Neil Cooper, Olivia Lunsford, Katie Croushorn, Angela Croushorn, and Jasmine Smith. You guys looked great!

About the Author

Amy Croushorn is an interior designer, party stylist, and editor of Amy's Party Ideas, a popular party planning website. She lives in Auburn, Alabama, with her son, Cole.

Measurement Conversion Charts

VOLUME

US	METRIC
⅕ teaspoon (tsp)	1 ml
1 teaspoon (tsp)	5 ml
1 tablespoon (tbsp)	15 ml
1 fluid ounce (fl. oz.)	30 ml
⅕ cup	50 ml
¼ cup	60 ml
⅓ cup	80 ml
3.4 fluid ounces (fl. oz.)	100 ml
½ cup	120 ml
⅔ cup	160 ml
¾ cup	180 ml
1 cup	240 ml
1 pint (2 cups)	480 ml
1 quart (4 cups)	.95 liter

WEIGHT

US	METRIC
0.5 ounce (oz.)	14 grams (g)
1 ounce (oz.)	28 grams (g)
¼ pound (lb)	13 grams (g)
⅓ pound (lb)	151 grams (g)
½ pound (lb)	227 grams (g)
1 pound (lb)	454 grams (g)

TEMPERATURES

FAHRENHEIT	CELSIUS
200°	93.3°
212°	100°
250°	121°
275°	135°
300°	149°
325°	165°
350°	177°
400°	205°
425°	220°
450°	233°
475°	245°
500°	260°

Recipe Index

Notes

INSIGHT
EDITIONS

PO Box 3088
San Rafael, CA 94912
www.insighteditions.com

Find us on Facebook: www.facebook.com/InsightEditions
Follow us on Twitter: @insighteditions

Library of Congress Cataloging-in-Publication Data available.

ISBN: 978-1-68383-654-4

Publisher: Raoul Goff
President: Kate Jerome
Associate Publisher: Vanessa Lopez
Creative Director: Chrissy Kwasnik
Designer: Judy Wiatrek Trum
Editor: Hilary VandenBroek
Editorial Assistant: Gabby Vanacore
Senior Production Editor: Elaine Ou
Managing Editor: Lauren LePera
Senior Production Manager: Greg Steffen
Production Manager: Eden Orlesky

Photo Credits
Amy Luigart Stayner: Pages 2, 10–57, 74–105, 136–149, 168–183, 188
Becky Sharp: Pages 6, 58–73, 106–135, 150–167, 184, 186
Jean Allsop: Cover

ROOTS of PEACE   REPLANTED PAPER

Insight Editions, in association with Roots of Peace, will plant two trees for
each tree used in the manufacturing of this book. Roots of Peace is an
internationally renowned humanitarian organization dedicated to eradicating
land mines worldwide and converting war-torn lands into productive farms
and wildlife habitats. Roots of Peace will plant two million fruit and nut trees in
Afghanistan and provide farmers there with the skills and support necessary
for sustainable land use.

Manufactured in China by Insight Editions

10 9 8 7 6